FROM STRAW TO PILLAR

Lyn Bair

From Straw to Pillar

A Pathway to Perfection as Taught in the Epistle of James

TATE PUBLISHING
AND ENTERPRISES, LLC

From Straw to Pillar
Copyright © 2012 by Lyn Bair. All rights reserved.

No part of this publication may be reproduced, stored in a retrieval system or transmitted in any way by any means, electronic, mechanical, photocopy, recording or otherwise without the prior permission of the author except as provided by USA copyright law.

Scripture quotations marked (AMP) are taken from the Amplified Bible, Copyright © 1954, 1958, 1962, 1964, 1965, 1987 by The Lockman Foundation. Used by permission.

Scripture quotations marked (KJV) are taken from the Holy Bible, King James Version, Cambridge, 1769. Used by permission. All rights reserved.

Scripture quotations marked (NIV) are taken from the Holy Bible, New International Version®, NIV®. Copyright © 1973, 1978, 1984 by Biblica, Inc.™ Used by permission of Zondervan. All rights reserved worldwide. www.zondervan.com

Scripture quotations marked (NRSV) are from New Revised Standard Version Bible, copyright © 1989 National Council of the Churches of Christ in the United States of America. Used by permission. All rights reserved..

The opinions expressed by the author are not necessarily those of Tate Publishing, LLC.

Published by Tate Publishing & Enterprises, LLC
127 E. Trade Center Terrace | Mustang, Oklahoma 73064 USA
1.888.361.9473 | www.tatepublishing.com

Tate Publishing is committed to excellence in the publishing industry. The company reflects the philosophy established by the founders, based on Psalm 68:11,
"The Lord gave the word and great was the company of those who published it."

Book design copyright © 2012 by Tate Publishing, LLC. All rights reserved.
Cover design by Rodrigo Adolfo
Interior design by Blake Brasor

Published in the United States of America

ISBN: 978-1-62147-552-1
1. Religion, Biblical Studies, New Testament
2. Religion, Christian Life, Personal Growth
12.10.18

DEDICATION

To my husband, Michael, without whom I would be quite incomplete, and to our children: C-pher, Erin, and Drew, may we continue our search for wholeness as an eternal family. Thank you all for providing a fertile proving ground for testing and trying these ideas.

And to Mom and Dad, thanks for raising me and teaching me the gospel of Jesus Christ since infancy. You are both remembered daily. To Art and Krista, I continue to have wonderful spiritual conversations and opportunities for personal growth with you both, my older siblings.

ACKNOWLEDGMENTS

I want to thank the following people, without whom this book would never have come into existence:

To my immediate and extended family members and to my dear friends: B, Robin, Sally, and Karen, I would not be who I am now without your unconditional love.

To the members of my congregations in Short Hills and Aspen, though you are too many to mention by name, I appreciate the gospel discussions and hours of service given on my behalf.

To the staff and students of Bridges High School, you are amazing! Thank you for your faith in my ideas and leadership. You inspire me daily to seek for something bigger than myself.

Special thanks to Angel and Brent for reading my manuscript and giving me specific feedback and ideas for its refinement.

Thanks to my editor, Hillary, for hearing my voice, and to all Tate Publishing staff members who helped me get my book to print: Carrie, Rachael, Lauren, Katja, Lisa, and many others.

TABLE OF CONTENTS

Introduction	9
Commentary on the Text of the Epistle	19
Chapter One	20
Chapter Two	42
Chapter Three	55
Chapter Four	60
Chapter Five	64
First Principle: Faith	77
Emulation	80
Admiration	87
Reasoned Conviction	94
Faith and Prayer	104
Seeking Light and Truth	113
Light: James Deals with Contemporary Religion and Scholarship	114
Truth: James Addresses Current Conventions of Thought	121
Light and Truth: James's Innovation and Enlightened Expression	125
Finding Current Application of James's Challenge	132

Living the Whole (Royal) Law (of Liberty)	141
The Law of Moses	146
The Law of Liberty	150
The Royal Law	155
Lessons by Example: Abraham, Rahab, Job, and Elijah	163
Who Are These People?	164
First Things First	168
Pivotal Moments	168
Four Keys to Freedom	170
Trials Make Us Stronger	171
"Control" Is Not Always a Bad Thing	179
Being Doers of the Word	191
Endnotes	207

INTRODUCTION

> Ideals are stars to steer by. They are not sticks to beat ourselves with.
>
> —Barbara B. Smith[1]

I often turn to great pieces of literature to find messages, possible paths to follow, and even to find answers to different situations. The method I use is far from scientific, I simply hold a book in my hands, look at the fore edge of the pages, close my eyes, offer a prayer seeking inspiration, and then release my hold on the book and let it fall open, believing somewhere on the randomly exposed pages there will be a message for me.

Doesn't seem like a perfect way to find answers, does it? A perfect method might be explained as being systematic: a process so clear and specific that each step can be repeated and the same results can be achieved each time the method is followed. Perfect or not, this is a process I often employ.

And so it was one day, when I grabbed the Bible to read something inspiring. The Scriptures dropped open to the Epistle of James, and I read James 1:22-24: "But be ye doers of the word, and not hearers only.... For if any be a hearer of the word, and not a doer, he is like unto a man beholding his natural face in a glass: For he beholdest himself, and goeth his way, and straightway forgetteth what manner of man he was."

I have read the Bible many times. As a child, my family set aside time every week for us to read from the scriptures and to talk about what different passages meant. I admit, I was not always a willing participant, but as I grew older this was an important bonding time for our family. During my senior year of high school, I asked my mother to answer some serious questions for me: where should I go to college and what should I study? Her response: "Remember what Jehoshaphat did with the people of Judah…?"[2] Yes, my mother answered my questions by instructing me to search the scriptures and listen to God. At the time I didn't really appreciate the method, but as I have raised my own children, I admit, it is a pretty handy way to give an answer without telling anyone exactly what to do. And there is an added benefit: our children learn to return to the Word of God to find answers to their own questions.

As I read this passage from James, I thought about the words as my parents might teach them and several more questions rushed into my mind. Could it be that in all my church attendance and participation, I was really only a hearer? I'm a pretty good doer, I thought, but what was my motivation for all my righteous activity? As I started to ponder these questions more reflectively, I had a very clear thought, I was doing everything expected by society, but I was the daughter of the King of heaven, and I had forgotten what manner of woman I am. As I looked at the pages of my study Bible, I realized very little was marked or highlighted in the Epistle of James, as if I had never really read and studied this book. I mention this only because for three decades I have taken college courses on the Bible, participated in Bible study groups, and taught both youth and adult Sunday school classes. I like to be prepared for class, so early in the week, I read and write questions about the scriptural passage to be discussed. During the week I look for applications of the text in my daily comings and goings. I also read other books looking for help to understand the history, topic, and lessons more clearly. Then, before I teach I prepare an outline of the lesson complete with historical and geographical notes, personal stories, important commentary, and scriptural references.

Given this somewhat anal-retentive approach to personal scripture study, imagine my own surprise when there were no study notes in my copy of the Epistle of James. How could I have overlooked this book so many times over the years? Well, it became clear, if I wanted to answer the reflective question: what manner of woman am I, I needed to study James.

Being a student of the twenty-first century, I went to the Internet and googled "The Epistle of James" to begin my study. Of course, the first reference displayed was a wiki page, *not a bad place to start*, I thought. As I was reading along I learned that historically there has been a debate over whether the Epistle of James should have been canonized. Eventually I read a quote from Martin Luther, "St James' Epistle is really an epistle of straw…for it has nothing of the nature of the gospel about it."[3] An epistle of straw, well I'm fascinated!

The Epistle of James, with its five short chapters, is tucked away toward the end of the New Testament. This small canonized book has been studied from many different points of view, sometimes rejected and sometimes embraced. A major criticism of the epistle says James is too closely connected and, therefore, tied to Jewish tradition, specifically with the tradition of wisdom literature. "There is nothing in the thought and teaching of James that does not find resonance in the world of Judaism. In fact, the theological stance of James is consistent with the basic theological perspectives of Judaism."[4] James clearly demonstrates his knowledge and familiarity with the Law of Moses throughout his epistle, often stating things in near mimic quality to passages found in the books of Exodus, Leviticus, and Deuteronomy. James also displays his general knowledge of Scripture as he quotes and makes unmistakable references to several other passages found in the Old Testament. But none of this scriptural knowledge prevents James from going beyond the Old Testament verses he refers to; in fact, he challenges his readers to regain familiarity with scriptures that perhaps were studied previously, for our author has already internalized the principles he presents.

The identity of James, the author, has been debated since early Christian times. A very compelling argument supports that "internal evidence" (contents of the epistle, its style, address, date, and place of composition) points unmistakably to James, the Lord's brother, the bishop of Jerusalem, as the author; he exactly, and he alone, fulfills the conditions required in the writer of the epistle."[5] Growing up as the brother of Jesus would have allowed James "constant intercourse with Him who was full of grace and truth, in childhood as in manhood,"[6] and this would have helped James find the Torah offering excellent direction for outward regulation, and Jesus offering an inner law of liberty. Our author, James, is referenced in the twelfth chapter of the Acts of the Apostles. The scene involved both the terrible news of the death of James the Apostle and the miraculous delivery of Peter from the hands of Herod. When Peter was reunited with other followers, he instructed someone to immediately go and inform James.[7] Later in the fifteenth chapter of Acts, Paul came to Jerusalem to settle a theological debate with church leaders. At this meeting Peter spoke first and then his words were confirmed by and expounded upon by James who quoted a passage from the Old Testament in support of Peter's decision.[8] In his epistle to the Galatians, Paul refers to this same James as a pillar of the church.[9] Having a letter written by such a knowledgeable author and "the Lord's brother is akin to having one penned by the Master himself. And in this general epistle, we find the son of Joseph, often in language reminiscent of that used by the son of Mary, setting forth the practical operation of the doctrines taught by his…brother."[10]

In my study of the Epistle of James, I decided to regain familiarity with scriptures I had previously studied and determine for myself why so many scholars criticize this tiny letter. The Interpreter's Bible claims The Epistle of James "not only represented a use of

Jewish tradition, but was Jewish tradition and nothing else."[11] At first this comment is extremely critical of a book found in the New Testament, if it fails to really speak of Christ, then why include it? However, if we place the twenty-seven books of the New Testament in chronological order, this epistle may be the first to be written. And then it seems quite natural; the Epistle of James is the first truly Christian document coming out of Jerusalem, and it is strongly connected to Jewish tradition. Obviously, there isn't a Christian tradition yet, and James has only stories from Jewish tradition and the words of Jesus as he experienced them as his sources. If we allow ourselves the possibility that this epistle is written by the brother of Jesus, we can begin to see new applications provided by the teachings of Jesus to those who were already living the Law of Moses. James seems to have been well trained in Judaism, and although he refers to many basic principles, all are presented with a new twist—a twist accounted for by his listening to and sharing space with the Lord Jesus Christ.

I like what some scholars have expressed about the style of this epistle "reminds one now of the Proverbs, now of the stern denunciations of the prophets, now of the parables in the Gospels,"[12] explaining "the understructure of James's theology is the wisdom of Jesus, as our Lord, the Savior taught it and lived it."[13] Additionally, the wisdom of James "represents the redemptive-historical realization of wisdom expressed directly by Jesus himself."[14] And "James's path to perfection and the Savior's teachings in the Sermon on the Mount in Matthew" have several parallels.[15] James has clearly synthesized the information learned from his Hebrew education with conversations he had with his family members. James sees the need for completeness in our lives, and he explains this idea as a combination of the Law of Moses and the inner purification preached by Jesus.

Today the five chapters of James in my study Bible are considerably marked and highlighted. I love this text. James speaks without reference to time or place, thereby allowing me to feel as if he wrote to me. James provides straightforward and simple advice on how to seek the lofty goal of perfection (first given by Christ in the Sermon on the Mount). It's a little overwhelming to think about an idea as extreme as perfection without getting a little depressed, especially if you have a tendency, like me, to compare yourself to *all* the successful people in the world. I'll never look like Catherine Zeta-Jones. I'll never have the elegance of Oprah. I'll never have the presence of General Colin Powell. In short, "I'll never..." is an easy way to put myself down and avoid striving for any improvement at all, let alone the ideal.

And perhaps most revealing to me through my study, James provides one of the earliest testimonies of the Redeemer of Israel, the Savior of the World and the power of His atonement. Indeed, if this is true, then the Old Testament is full of stories and explanations of the atonement, many of which James cites. Thus, instead of criticizing James for providing a book of Jewish tradition, we could embrace him for declaring the Jewish tradition with its focus on Jesus Christ, the Messiah. I recognize that at one point in my life, I was perhaps a bit like Martin Luther, as I viewed the Epistle of James to have little to no value, *it was to me straw*. But now I feel a strength from the text that builds my own testimony of the Savior, *it is to me a pillar*.

In our study of the Epistle of James, let us explore the chapters, verses, and words of the epistle and attempt to see opportunities to apply its message in our daily lives, just as James applied the message of Jesus in his. Let us discard our partiality and instead seek for spiritual maturity. Let us discard the thoughts of inadequacy and simply be intrigued and desirous about believing in the possibility of achieving some ideal or indeed perfection. Let us begin a journey of seeking perfection and of rediscovering who we really are.

Throughout the book, we will pause to reflect on various ideas. There are many examples where individual things are not particularly strong by themselves: twine, straw, people, even ideas. However, when these items are collected and bundled together they have a very strong nature: twine weaves into rope, straw is baled and can be stacked, people form communities, and ideas make more sense upon reflection. Take some time to think about and answer the following questions. You may wish to use these as starter questions with a small group or during a Bible study.

Sorting and Bundling: Integrative Questions for Reflection

What are the advantages in accepting the half-brother of Jesus as the author of the epistle?

What do you know about this epistle? When was the Epistle of James written? When did it become part of the New Testament canon?

What are the main topics taught in this epistle?

What does perfection mean to you?

Do you think seeking perfection is a realistic goal? Why or why not?

What might happen to your feelings and ideas about the subject if the word *perfection* were exchanged for *spiritual maturity*?

Is seeking spiritual maturity something you desire?

Lyn Bair

COMMENTARY ON THE TEXT OF THE EPISTLE

> Reading is…the royal road to intellectual eminence…. Truly good books are more than mines to those who can understand them. They are the breathings of the great souls of past times. Genius is not embalmed in them, but lives in them perpetually.
>
> —William Ellery Channing [16]

Like many others, I have also expressed mild frustration in reading difficult texts. Often, it is because the language is time-specific and, therefore, somewhat beyond casual reading. Sometimes I dare say, "I'm just not that into it." In essence, difficult texts need time for study, thought, and conversation.

A few summers ago I took the opportunity to attend a Summer Classics seminar at St. John's College in Santa Fe, NM. Although I had previously studied the work and writing of Leonardo da Vinci, I decided to read a new copy of the primary work on which the seminar would focus, suspending past understanding and prejudices. So I read and tried to understand each of the assigned readings anew. During the seminar sessions, we would view and discuss Leonardo's work. In listening to the group's conversation, my personal study and thinking about the *Art of Painting* expanded.

So it is with Scripture. The Holy Bible can be a difficult text to read and understand. My understanding of the Bible has been benefited by taking classes, attending book and study groups, attending Sunday school, and even listening to lectures on related topics. All of these supportive environments add to the enjoyment and potential understanding of what I read. Without experiencing community conversation, I cannot hear the wisdom of my peers. Even though I commit to personal study time, if I forget to include a period of meditation and time for reflective thought, I cannot truly hear the voices of the inspired biblical authors nor grasp the important meanings and messages contained on the pages of Scripture.

I would like to investigate the text of James's epistle from this attitude. Instead of rehearsing all the scholarship offered on the subject for two millennia, I would like to investigate the text and delve into how this epistle can help us live the gospel both in principle and in practice to see if it offers guidance to seek perfection.

James Chapter One
James 1:1

In his opening verse, James introduces himself and reveals the intended audience of his letter. It is important that he claims to be a servant of God and of his Lord, Jesus Christ. There are two Greek words translated as servant: δουλος and θεραπων. While *doulos* (δουλος) can be used to simply show enslavement, it

From Straw to Pillar

also suggests not merely a servant but one in a permanent relationship. *Therapon* (θεραπων) can be used to describe the action of serving, attending, and flattering, or it can describe one whose services are more tender, nobler, and purer than those of the doulos. In today's world we think negatively about the term *servant*, perhaps as one who is merely obedient to his master and has no freedoms. I think James's usage is more like what would be seen in the Old Testament, for example, when the Lord explains the difference between His relationship with "a prophet among you" and with His "servant Moses."[17] God blesses both, but with Moses He speaks "mouth to mouth" and not just in dreams and visions. Thus, when James calls himself a servant, it is not a derogatory title but one that shows his close relationship, tender feelings, and attentiveness to God. In this opening then, James expresses his desired connection to God and to Jesus Christ; in other words, he declares himself to be a disciple. As we will discover, his epistle is filled with instructions about how we, individually and in a community, can become disciples.

James addresses his letter to the twelve tribes of Israel scattered abroad, or those not living in the homeland of Palestine. At the time James wrote his epistle, ten of the twelve tribes had already been scattered and thus were living outside of Palestine. Perhaps James thought it wise to write to these children of Israel because they might not have had full knowledge of the events that had occurred during the life of Jesus nor a full account of His teachings. Since not all of the scattered Israelites were necessarily living in the same place, James is also addressing a group of people whose location he does not know. He writes, therefore, in a prophetic manner, understanding what the Lord needs him to relate to His people but unaware of the method or the time his letter will be delivered. It seems possible that James, like Isaiah, needed to write to both current saints and saints of the future at the same time. This is the second time James follows a pattern from the Old Testament; first he follows it in his usage of the word *servant* and then how he addresses his audience.

In writing to his audience, members of the twelve tribes, James issues a challenge for them to become perfect and whole, and in return, he promises they will "[want] nothing." The message of James's epistle is very similar to a story about Moses and the "House of Jacob"[18] prior to the delivery of the Ten Commandments.[19] The children of Israel are camped in the wilderness near Sinai. Moses seeks instruction from God and is told the words he should deliver: "Ye have seen what I did unto the Egyptians, and how I bare you on eagles wings, and brought you unto myself. Now therefore, if ye will obey my voice indeed, and keep my covenants, then ye shall be a peculiar treasure unto me above all people...." When presented with this invitation, "all the people answered together, and said, 'All that the Lord hath spoken we will do.'" In this story, the Lord offered the children of Israel a covenant, an agreement, with a blessing: be obedient, and I will make you a powerful kingdom. God, through His prophets, Moses and James, offers nearly the same covenant to His children to be obedient always (become perfect), and you will be powerful (want nothing).

Also important with regard to this first verse is to consider the author's name: James. We know that in the King James Version of the Bible, the name "Jacob" remained as Jacob in the Old Testament, but in the New Testament, Jacob was consistently changed to James. If our author's true name was actually Jacob, then the fact that he writes a letter to the twelve tribes of Israel is extremely significant. Israel is not only a location but also the name of the father of the twelve tribes. Remember Jacob's name was changed to Israel[20] when God renewed the Abrahamic covenant with him. Thus, our author writes his message prophetically, also by name, to his own people and speaking as a father would advise his own children. Here again, James follows an Old Testament format evident when fathers give blessings to their children prior to their death. This reality makes the message James offers historical, paternal, and tender.

James 1:2-4

In this next group of verses, James reminds us all that trials are a natural part of mortal life and that our attitude about these difficulties needs to be positive. The meaning of the Greek words in verse 3 suggests, we gain approval from God by triumphing in trials. This testing brings about faith and helps to produce abilities that encourage endurance, and endurance works toward wholeness or perfection. Throughout the epistle, James gives examples of what the "temptations" might look like: "sinful speech, disobedience, unconcerned about others, worldliness, quarreling, arrogance and evil inclinations toward the rich."[21] But at the same time, James continues to provide reasons why we should strive for perfection. He explains that there is a process of growth: "trials test faith; the testing of faith promotes endurance; endurance, if it is continued till it attains it end, builds up the perfectly matured Christian character."[22] Regardless of the temptations we have, there is a path we can take to help us be whole.

During Christ's ministry, He heals a variety of people. In one instance, as told by John, He heals a man who has had an infirmity for thirty-eight years by asking, "Wilt thou be made whole?" and then says, "Rise, take up thy bed, and walk." Later, when questioned about why the man was carrying his bed on the Sabbath, he explains, "He that made me whole, the same said unto me, Take up thy bed and walk."[23] The word choice in this story connects the idea of being healed with being made whole, which are words not only used by the Savior but by the man who had an infirmity as well. Certainly this infirmity was a trial, and though he went through the process, like many others, of trying to be healed by entering the pool of Bethesda, he had never been able. Now when asked if he wanted to be whole, he explained that he would, but there was no one to help him get to the healing waters. The man believed the waters had power to heal his infirmity, and he had endured his trial and his attempts to be healed for many years. Finally, his desire to be whole is granted through the words of the Savior. These are the same steps James relates to us in these verses, introducing the idea of becoming perfect, whole, and like God. James's imperative statement in verse 4 is parallel to Christ's statement from the Sermon on the Mount: "Be ye therefore perfect, even as your Father which is in heaven is perfect."[24]

Perfection is often translated from the Greek *telos* (τελος), interpreted as "fulfillment," "fully," or "to the end."[25] If we look at this pursuit of perfection as an opportunity and process to spiritually mature and fulfill our missions, even if on a daily basis, we can begin to accept the challenge offered by both James and the Savior. If we are willing to work toward spiritual maturity or spiritual wholeness, then we are working toward integrity and, therefore, perfection.

My parents held high expectations for all their children. They expected us to help around the house and do our chores well and on schedule. They expected us to not get into trouble at school but learn and produce satisfactory work for our teachers. They expected (and provided a way) that each of us would attend a university and graduate with at least a bachelor's degree. And when we started our own families, they expected us to continue to include them in our lives (visits, holidays, photos, letters, and so forth). Everything my parents expected was doable even if at times what they hoped for felt beyond my current abilities.

Sometimes when I read James's admonitions, I can hear my parents providing needed—but not always appreciated—counsel. I remember calling my father once during college to complain about where I was and hoping that he would allow me to come home. His response seemed harsh at the time, but it now strikes me as very wise. He counseled, "You are at a good school, you have fine professors, and you know how to learn and study. Now do the job you have been sent to do." When I read James's message in these terms, I hear my father's voice, and I understand more personally what James bluntly states in his epistle.

James 1:5-8

After introducing the idea of wholeness or perfection, James provides his first suggestion of how we can make the goal a reality: seek wisdom. James's audience "is wavering in their faith in the face of persecution, he is reminding them of the tradition that will support them. That tradition is one of developing insight into God's way"[26] through seeking wisdom. We learn too that it is acceptable and even encouraged for us to ask God questions directly and to seek direction and wisdom from Him, for He will not turn us away. James identifies the pursuit of wisdom as an important tool we can use to be victorious over trials and temptations.[27]

> In biblical times the word *wisdom* (Hebrew *hokma*) had a very narrow meaning as well as a general meaning. The confined definition of wisdom was associated with the demonstration of a person's dexterity in a skill or in an art.... The more general meaning of the word was identified with intelligence, sensibility, judiciousness, with reason, and skillful to judge. [28]

When experiencing difficult circumstances, who would not want to be able to reason skillfully and arrive at sound decisions?

To gain this wisdom where we reason well and make good decisions, James tells us our faith must not waver, nor can we be double-minded but that we must move forward with wholeness or integrity. Seeking wisdom then requires an action grounded in faith; we ask God for guidance without wavering in our purpose. "The predominating sense in which the term *faith* is used throughout the Scriptures is that of full confidence and trust in the being, purposes, and words of God."[29] It appears the laws of Newton have meaning to our use of faith, in that an object at rest will remain at rest unless acted upon; in other words, our faith will not grow or increase if we do nothing but believe. And the action James encourages us to take is to ask God for enough wisdom to make reasonable and sound judgment in our daily actions.

These verses also teach that if we are undecided about our course, we will not receive all the blessings we might have received had we acted with full purpose of heart and committed to our resolve. We learn God is constant and eternal and will do as He has promised, but we as human beings are not typically steadfast. James wants the readers of his letter to "understand that God responds to us only when our lives reflect a basic consistency of purpose and intent: a spiritual integrity."[30] Because this letter is addressed to the twelve tribes, perhaps James is also reminding us of the covenant God made with Abraham, a covenant that the children of Israel were entitled to. The fulfillment of this covenant includes the restoration of the twelve tribes, bringing all tribes back from where they have been dispersed.

Remember that James addresses his epistle to the twelve tribes in dispersion. Perhaps then, he is providing the light that needs to be followed to come out of captivity and bondage so that all tribes can participate in the blessings of the covenant. James will specifically mention Abraham and use his life as an example of what it means to have wisdom and act on our faith (2:21-24), but his intention in these verses is to introduce the need for us to seek light. If James is writing also to modern-day Christians, then it would be important to remind them that the Abrahamic covenant also promises that the Spirit of God would be among the Gentiles and because of their membership in God's church, they also would be heirs to the blessings of the Abrahamic covenant.[31] In fact, they would be significant participants in helping the twelve tribes to be restored. James then is connecting Christians to Old Testament scripture, demonstrating how we can help fulfill the purposes of God.

James 1:9-12

Humility seems to be the theme of verses 9-12. James suggests that we learn best when we are humble and that in our humble circumstances, we are more apt to listen and have a wider perspective. James exhorts the humble members of the community "to look toward their spiritual identity as the measure of their ultimate significance."[32] He explains that when we become proud (of our intellect or possessions), we have lost the perspective that things are temporary. When we are proud, we operate from a position of comparison (we are better than or we have more skills). When we believe that we are superior, we have lost our humility. Humility can be seen in many settings of modern life; one with particular difficulties is university life. Here, the disciples of Christ are criticized as being too humble, mere sheep, willing to follow without intellectual challenging. And yet the history of the Christian scholar demonstrates that choosing to follow Christ is an active, thought-filled course, not "some kind of blind faith, but rather a commitment based on personal appreciation of the value and efficacy of the spiritual path."[33]

In a recent gathering of Christian students in New Haven, the speaker reminded them that "…one who sees the truth must live bearing witness to it. In some classes there is a feeling that truly intelligent people are not people of great faith."[34] Thus, when we declare our affiliation with Christ and His people, others may choose to criticize and question our intelligence. The "educated" world does not often give merit or value to such a humble position as being a follower, even when we are followers of the Lord, Jesus Christ. Seeking to be made whole through the Savior then is a very humbling experience; perfection is a goal worth enduring.

Once we commit to the path of seeking perfection, we quickly realize that "progress can be hard to recognize, especially if our expectations are unrealistically high."[35] Perfection is the loftiest of goals. If we were going to climb a mountain peak, we would do many things to prepare. We might read about various routes that others have taken, learning about the trail markers and geographic features. We certainly would plan ahead with water and food. We would want to have the best clothing and equipment, being prepared for sudden changes in weather. We would want to be sure to allow enough time for us to reach our goal successfully. And each time we attempted to reach a new apex, we would learn a little bit more about ourselves. Seeking perfection is a lot like preparing for this mountain ascent, and James is trying to provide us with some of the proper tools, guides, trail markers, and the equipment we need on our journey. All of the experience, strength, and hope I have accumulated are within me today, guiding my choices. I may not recognize it right now, but I have made progress. If I am learning something I have learned before; I must need to know it more deeply. As we seek perfection, we sooner or later learn to measure our progress in smaller units. We also learn that we need help and support from a power much greater than ourselves; James declares that the power we need is to be sought from God Himself.

In these verses James also warns us about being overly concerned about the outward appearance of things. When the message of the verses from the first half of chapter one is looked to in total, we begin to understand that wealth and power are not the constant things upon which we should focus but that we should spend our energies searching for wisdom and showing faithfulness and the ability to stay true to our intentions. We need to become rich in our association with Christ while remaining aware of our human frailties. We need to allow our inner spirituality to be more important than the outward show of social status.

James also introduces us to the idea of respecting people. Respect for others is a positive attribute because we show our deep affection or admiration for their skills, qualities, and/or accomplishments. Respect, as used in the Scriptures, is usually synonymous with reverence. However, as James would have been familiar, Moses taught us not to be respecters of people. "Ye shall do no unrighteousness in judgment: thou shalt not respect the person of the poor, nor honour the person of the mighty...."[36] "Ye shall not respect persons in judgment; but ye shall hear the small as well as the great; ye shall not be afraid of the face of man; for the judgment is God's: and the cause that is too hard for you, bring it unto me, and I will hear it."[37] In both cases, we are warned not to make unrighteous judgments based on what we classify as poor or mighty, small or great; do not be a respecter of others.

A story about King David and his family is instructive. King David's house was suffering because of his personal sins. His oldest son, Amnon, had sexually forced himself upon his half-sister, Tamar, and then rejected and despised her. Absalom was filled with hate about the incident and plotted to kill his brother Amnon. After accomplishing the deed, Absalom fled from his father's anger, and the two (father and son) were separated for at least two years. David's nephew and army captain, Joab, sought reconciliation between

David and Absalom, finally enlisting the help of a "wise woman."[38] She presented a dilemma to the king and asked for protection. The story she related was that one of her sons had killed the other, and the community now sought to punish the living son. Such a death would leave the widow without any posterity. She said, "For we must needs die, and are as water spilt on the ground, which cannot be gathered up again; neither doth God respect any person: yet doth he devise means, that his banished be not expelled from him."[39] In asking for protection and forgiveness for her son, she simultaneously asked the king to protect and forgive his own son, and to find some way that the two could be reconciled. The wise woman asked the king to not be a respecter of persons.

The lesson we can learn is that regardless of what we do, God wants us all to return to Him, and He has, therefore, created ways and means for us to accomplish that task. James encourages our endurance to become whole—as we struggle through the ups and downs of life, searching for the means to return to God. Then in verse 12, James repeats the invitation he offered in verses 2-4. This time the promise of endurance and seeking perfection is expressed as receiving "the crown of life."

James 1:13-18

Here, a pattern of rhetoric is used to convince us to James's cause. He contrasts two pieces of information, hoping to persuade us to the one course he believes is wiser. James presents the first of these two contrasting points and talks about the behavior of man in verses 13-16. He points out to his audience that we tend to blame others for our problems. He says in verse 13, "Let no man say when he is tempted, I am tempted of God...." If we think we are simply victims of God when in temptation, then we do not understand the truth, and we have deceived ourselves. "The common threads of how self-deceived persons see themselves and their circumstances include, not surprisingly, a sense of being helpless in the face of what others are doing to them. This view swallows up any sense of personal responsibility for creating or perpetuating the problem and obliterates the possibility that they are participating in any way in a willful refusal to walk in the light."[40] James is urging us to accept personal responsibilities for our actions—both inner thoughts and outer actions. He wants us to see temptation for what it is and not use it as an excuse to not seek God.

In verses 17-18, James presents his counterargument and contrasts the actions of man with the behavior of God. He explicitly states two qualities of God, light and truth, and assures us that God wants these things for all of His children. James states clearly that we need to recognize the source of our blessings and that we should know that goodness comes from God and that He would have us love and serve each other.

James 1:19-21

James wants us to make a commitment of heart and mind. For him, certain behaviors stop us from seeking light and truth. By presenting a series of ideas that are in opposition to each other, James shows us a path that, if taken, can bring us to a better way of life. Often his "opposites" are not obvious, and we may need to consider how the two ideas work together and against each other. For example, James pairs "swift to hear" with "slow to speak." Most of us, if asked, would probably say the opposite of swift is slow, but how many of us would respond that the opposite of hearing is speaking? When we consider the pair "swift to hear" and "slow to speak," we begin to think about the possible advantages of listening to others. Scientific research tells us "we literally only hear what we listen for. We pay special attention to what we are expecting to see, hear, feel, or taste…. When you listen to people, unless you consciously choose a certain way to listen, you will listen to prove your existing theories…."[41]

Even when we employ skills known as "active listening," we only listen a small percentage of the time because the major part of our listening is really spent predicting, assessing, judging, and figuring out a way to make ourselves sound smart when we finally speak. The listening that James is encouraging us to do is to support others. We support others by providing a sounding board for them to work through their ideas aloud, while believing that they already have all the tools necessary to succeed.[42] When we are expecting to hear certain ideas and preparing to jump into the conversation with our own ideas, we are missing the opportunity to encourage and love others. James pairs "swift to hear" also with "slow to anger." Although at first, these two ideas don't feel at odds, I think about the times that I listen to newscasts and get angry or insulted by what is reported, and I think, *Yeah, I hear and get offended.* I also think about times when I hear one side of a story and really try to imagine what the other side could sound like, trying to empathize with another person and their situation. In this second scenario, I am a different person. I become thoughtful and tolerant and look for peaceful solutions. I tend to be concerned for more than just myself, and I take less physical action, investing instead contemplation and hope for others to experience peace. I think this is who James is trying to get us to become.

James's next opposing ideas are: "Lay apart all filthiness" and "Receive with meekness the engrafted word." I understand the lay apart and receive pairing as being opposites, but again, who would suggest that the opposite of filthiness was meekness? I think James is trying to get us to understand that when we are caught up in unrighteous thoughts and actions that we are not meek and humble, and we are, therefore, not willing to hear or change. And thus James's new ideas reconnect to his first thought: "swift to hear." James's emphasis on hearing as opposed to speech or anger "teaches us the need for openheartedness. For without it, we have no room to receive the blessings and positive transformation that we might otherwise experience in our interaction with our fellow human beings."[43] Instead of continuing to act in ways that are not helping us become spiritually mature, we need to welcome the more peaceful ways of God. "Almost all of us...fail to lighten our load for the long and arduous journey of discipleship. We fail to put off the childish things—not the Tinkertoys, but the temper tantrums; not the training pants, but pride. We remain unnecessarily burdened by things which clearly should and can be jettisoned."[44]

Verse 21 uses the word *engrafted*. Paul preached about how the Gentiles are wild olive tree branches that are grafted to the tame olive trees representing the House of Israel that has strong roots and fatness.[45] Trees and branches are combined in a new way when they are grafted so that new, young wild shoots can grow stronger and tamer because of their association with the original tree and its root system. Through the allegory of the olive tree, Paul explains how the Gentiles are being engrafted and receiving the blessings of the gospel now and how the Jews will eventually be gathered again and accept their role as the original well-rooted tree or the covenant people. Here is yet another reference to how the Christian can share the blessings of the Abrahamic covenant. James seems to be suggesting a similar explanation when he tells us to accept the Word and make it part of our heart and minds, because if we covenant through the gospel with God, in return, we will be blessed by a power that will save us and make us immortal.

In terms of James's audience, he seems to now be speaking to the Gentiles who have chosen to be part of the Lord's vineyard. The Gentiles will first become stronger (richer) and eventually be able to return their strength to the people from the lost tribes of Israel as they return and are gathered back to God, because they were engrafted. This is a strong message for the tribes

From Straw to Pillar

of Israel that have been scattered and wonder about their status as the chosen people. And this is a strong message for future saints who will have a part to play in the gathering and converting of the chosen people from the lost tribes of Israel.

Imagine for a moment being raised believing that you are part of God's chosen people—people God has selected out from the rest and was willing to make covenants with. Your ancestral history is full of heavenly interventions and miracles, amazing victories over enemies who appeared more powerful, and individual forefathers who told of their conversations with deity. You would feel pretty special! But now, realize that you have been removed from this favored position, and although promised that God wants you back, the world seems totally against you. Then a group approaches you and proclaims that they are the current keepers of the covenant and that they want to help you and bring you back to your previous status as a member of God's covenant and chosen people. At first, you might think they were very misguided, and then you might feel confused, judged, and perhaps vulnerable. You might lash out, attacking others with words and actions. That's my briefest Christian summary of the history of the Jewish people and their present situation.

As a Christian, I also recognize that I, like the chosen people, have made a covenant with God to represent Him and help expand His kingdom on earth. Accepting that I am part of the wild olive trees that had the privilege to be engrafted into the old, tame, wise trees comes with an obligation. With my new vigor and understanding and hope, I must help the old tree see a new course. For the House of Israel, acknowledging vulnerability will only be possible "if [they] feel [they] can reach out for support. To do so, [they] must feel some competence in [their] relationships"[46] with other covenant people. We will be unable to fulfill our part if we are not people who others trust and feel safe with; we must be humble and wise, slow to speak and openhearted, unbiased and compassionate. We must be committed to God in heart and mind.

James 1:22-24

Always direct and to the point, James, in verses 22-24, gives another imperative "be ye doers of the word." This is another way for James to address the issue of integrity, reminding us that we must not be double-minded and hearers but not doers. James discussed consecration earlier in chapter one when he challenged the community to strive for wholeness. The second connection James gives is about obedience and listening, and listening becomes an element that facilitates our soul's embracing of the concepts. When we accept the concepts of the gospel fully, we become doers of the Word. The other part of the message in these verses is that what we see is not always real but often a mirror image. James reminds us about who we are on the inside; he recalls to our minds that we are the children of God and that inside we are spiritual beings. He not only encourages us to remember this fact but also directs us to act according to this truth.

James 1:25-27

The end of chapter one introduces the phrases "perfect law of liberty" and "pure religion." James will discuss these further in chapter two when he demonstrates his understanding of the Law of Moses as given in Leviticus and teaches that the law of liberty is God's complete law of accountability and agency. In the very last verse, James talks of "pure religion" in a way that equates it with charity, the pure love of Christ. These two new phrases show James's understanding that the words and ideas of the Old Testament can be understood anew through the words of Christ.

To summarize, the first chapter of the Epistle of James provides direction to individuals in a community that is struggling with challenges. James encourages the individual members of the community to raise their faith and actions to be more perfect. James teaches five important truths:

1. There is value in gaining experience, faith, and wisdom through trial.

2. We need to know our individual spiritual identities.

3. Our earthly missions are important to our salvation.

4. Opportunities come when we seek wisdom (light).

5. The power of the pure love of Christ can affect our lives (truth).

Before we turn to chapter two of James's epistle to see how the author develops the themes introduced, we pause to reflect. Take some time to review the first chapter of James and answer the following questions.

Sorting and Bundling:
Integrative Questions for Reflection

Think about one of the learning experiences you have had in your life. How difficult was it to live through? Have you experienced a heightened sense of understanding about this trial, maybe even a feeling of joy that you survived and learned something new about yourself?

How could you share your experiences of trials and overcoming trials with someone else to help build his or her faith?

Who are you? Write about the names that you have: the names given to you by your parents, nicknames given by those who love you, and names that witness a new level of commitment (perhaps adoption, new citizenship, or religious rites).

How does your collection of names affect your spiritual identity?

What would happen if you viewed your communication with God as an opportunity to change your heart and be transformed by His power?

Why is it important to know God will not upbraid or scold us for approaching Him in prayer?

Is there any difference between reciting prayers, speaking to God from the heart, or meditating? What are the strengths of these methods of communication with God?

Read a single verse of James and rewrite it in more common language. How does the idea of this verse relate to Jesus Christ?

_____

_____

_____

James Chapter Two

James 2:1-4

When first reading the opening verse of chapter two, it sounds like James criticizes our proclaimed faith. He questions our ability to believe in Christ while we continue to judge others. At first, I don't want to continue reading. I don't like his characterization of me (I told you that I try to liken the Scriptures to my life and situation). In fact, I begin to argue with the author. I try to be open to other people, to consider their situations and background, their needs and aspirations. But I also know that I judge. Is James telling me that I don't really believe in Christ because I naturally evaluate? I calm myself and think, *Let me not be offended but take in more verses of chapter two to see what point James is trying to make.*

Often verses are connected in chiastic literary style. If this is the case with verses 1-4, then verse 1 and verse 4 will help explain each other. Thus in the phrase, "Are ye not then partial in yourselves, and become judges of evil thoughts," James seems to set up a comparison, first, between the Lord of glory who is complete and our partial selves and, second, the differences between His judgments which honor people and ours that are not always so positive. James's attack (that I took personally) creates a tension that actually reveals the whole and complete nature of Christ's judgments of people. He sees beyond apparel and social standing. In contrast, our limited vision and abilities affect the judgments we make. Where Christ is perfect, we are partial. I totally agree.

James's explanation of our errors in judgment is not unlike instructions Moses gave the children of Israel. The Lord invites us, through Moses, to "be holy: for I the Lord your God am holy"[47] and then proceeds to instruct us about how to become more like Him. The lesson is further explained when we are instructed to not make unrighteous judgments of others based on their wealth or poverty, nor their honors and powers. This particular passage from the Old Testament may have been a major source of James's education, and, therefore, he is sharing personal insight based on his personal experience and his scriptural understandings.

Let me put this in personal, more modern terms. I want to be healthy and strong. But this desire has to be more than just an idea, I must put my desire into action. I tend to be a little skeptical of new programs, especially those that promise fabulous results with very little work on my part. So before I jump into something, I need to understand the value and merits of the program. Usually in my research, I discover many things, and then I must make a decision. Since I am already convinced that I should be healthy and strong, now I just need to find the best course. The message that James is sharing in these verses is similar. He suggests that if we accept the premises of his introduction: value of trials, knowing individual spiritual identities, achieving earthly missions, seeking wisdom, and loving others, then we understand the merits of trying to become perfect, mature, and whole. Now James needs to show us the best course for us to achieve this spiritual maturity and wholeness.

James 2:5-7

James's first example to persuade us on the path of following Christ and becoming more like him is to talk about the rich and the poor. First, he tells us that God chose the poor of the world because they were rich in faith. Then he reminds us that we despise the poor, or those that we perceive as being poorer than us. The very next statement asks us to reflect on how we are oppressed by people that are richer than we are and those that look down on us and judge us.

Recently I read a story online. The article was written by a man who was homeless between 1983-84. He talked about being given "the look," a judgment that he himself had probably given before to others in dire straits. He expressed his sadness of being on the receiving side of this humiliating stare.

The story is a modern-day James example. We tend to look down on people who appear different and poorer than we are at a given moment in time. We judge. But we judge the person and not just the situation or circumstances. We are making judgments of others based on appearances, while God accepts us based on our faith.

James accuses us of dishonoring the poor and not recognizing that what we do to some is very similar to what others have done to us. James's specific examples are about oppression, being called to court, and being made fun of because of associations. In verse 7 James talks of blasphemy, which is contemptuous speech about God or something that is believed to be sacred. Thus, the examples James provides about the rich oppressing and belittling the poor is a fairly wide condemnation of us when we judge others for their beliefs and practices.

I have traveled to the island of Patmos twice. On one occasion, I participated in a local tour that included the sanctuary where the Apostle John had received his revelation of the apocalypse. My tour guide, Athena, was a devout Christian. She shared with us doctrine from the stories about the life and teachings of the Apostle John. She urged us to be reverent when we visited the shrines. At one point, I admit I thought, *Whatever! What a tourist scam.* But then I asked my guide a question, and she answered quietly and with great sincerity. And there it was, my James moment: I had judged her for her belief and practice, for the situation I was in, but then I realized that she was a woman of great faith and that I needed to humble myself and be more willing to learn from her.

James 2:8-12

James next introduces the idea that when we do anything wrong and break even a small part of the law, we have failed completely. This sounds like a Satan argument, part true and part false. Yes, breaking a tiny part of the commandments can cause great sin and great loss, but that loss does not have to be an eternal loss. A small sin is just that—small—and committing a small error does not eliminate us from heaven as long as we pick ourselves up, repent, and start over.

Satan wants us to see perfection as always doing everything right: wearing the right clothes, saying the right things, impressing the right people, and, let's face it, that will never happen! It seems difficult to accept that an apostle would deliver an untruth, so what is James really suggesting?

Let's explore his rhetorical style, especially the device where he begins ideas with "but." In these cases, he seems to offer additional explanations or proofs. Applying this method to the respecting people passage (verses 5-7) as opposed to this passage, the royal law passage (verses 8-12), we can learn that to judge or respect people is a sin against the law. Thus, if we judge we sin, and therefore we understand the law because we transgress it and experience its consequences, whereas God is the only judge of the royal law, and until the final judgment occurs, we understand the royal law not by breaking it but by keeping it.

In this passage (verses 8-12) James introduces the terms *royal law, law,* and *law of liberty,* and he talks about them as if we completely understand the terminology, for he provides no further explanation. So, what might these terms mean? Interestingly, when we investigate weights and measures of James's time, we learn of "talents" that were typical coin units. There were royal talents and talents (common talents), where the royal weights or talents were about twice as valuable as the commonly used weights or talents. If the vocabulary is applied to law, the royal law would be twice what the common law is, thus something must be added to the law to make it equivalent to the royal law.

James mentions three laws: the Law of Moses, the law of liberty, and the royal law. He wants us to construct for ourselves the idea that the royal law is more valuable because it is made up of the law and the law of liberty. The common law for the Israelites was the Law of Moses. Keeping the whole law seems to refer to keeping all the commandments, keeping the statutes given in the Law of Moses, or doing proper actions. Keeping the law of liberty seems to be more about making good choices and about being consistent with those choices in both thought and action. Given these understandings, then, the double weight of the royal law would be accomplished by adding the law and the law of liberty together. Thus in the royal law, we become responsible for both doing the right things *and* choosing the right way. The royal law contains elements of both accountability and agency.

I believe that another understanding of the royal law comes if we consider how the three laws James talks about are connected to judgments. Consider that the law is akin to how humans judge. Our judgments are flawed and based on external appearance and our personal comparison with others and their actions. Now think about the royal law as a descriptor of how God judges. His judgments are based on looking beyond mere appearance; He looks at our hearts and our motives. Perhaps we want the liberty to be judged based on the law that gives us the best advantage, either our actions or our motives, whichever were judged as being better.

Then again, James's discussion could be relating still something different. What if the royal law is connected to King David or to Christ as the heir to the royal line of King David? Does such a connection equate the royal law with the law of heaven? What laws must God obey? Does this law explain God's purposes with regard to His children? Is the law of heaven an expansion of love thy neighbor to loving each individual and honoring each person for who they are (a child of God) and what they may become (more like Him)?

I realize I have more questions than answers, but finding the right questions to ask is truly at the heart of learning. As we grow and mature, the questions we ask change. As I learn more and form my opinions, I am influenced by many ideas, and I must discern truth and value of what I read and hear. For me, truth resonates. I have a tendency to mark text as I read. I underline and put vertical marks on longer passages that speak to me, and I also mark out or ex-out passages that do not ring true. My children have teased me about my system of textual notation, especially when they borrow my books and come across paragraphs that have been crossed out and where a less-than-flattering marginal comment has been added. I have read lots of books; many I have enjoyed, and they helped me gain understanding, while others were fun and were picked up to entertain. Still others were read and then discarded (well, put on the shelves in unflattering locations).

I have heard the opinion of some that if any part of a text is untrue, then the whole text is false. But personal experience and reading chapter two of James causes me to think differently; perhaps the stuff of human beings is partial, but the things of God are whole. Human books can offer partial truth while God's books offer the whole truth. Thus, when I read things written by fellow beings, I can look for the parts that are good and that offer positive direction and deeper understanding; and when I read Scripture, I need to align myself and my actions with the truths that are contained in the writing.

James 2:13-16

James now begins to provide specific examples of how the law differs from the royal law. It is often suggested that the Old Testament provides us details about how to conduct our daily lives and that we are supposed to find the greater meaning in our combined repetitive actions but that the New Testament provides the big ideas, and we determine our daily actions so as to prove we have understood the bigger picture. In essence, this is the difference between the Law of Moses and the Gospel of Christ. By providing additional examples, James is building an argument where the conclusion will be a need for the atonement. The lesser law exposes our hopelessness because the demands of justice are always met, whereas the royal law or atonement is a law where mercy can meet the demands of justice. Thus James's discussion on faith and works is similar to the justice and mercy argument. At first, both discussions seem at odds, but through the view of the gospel, we can explain their connection and harmony.

The discussion begun earlier is now partly disclosed. James did not suggest hopelessness when stating that if we fail in one part, we have failed in all; he was instead explaining the limits of the Law of Moses, whereas the royal law of atonement gives hope when parts of the law have been broken. James instructs us in verses 15-16 that we must give the right things to people in need, in fact, there is no value to us, or others, when we choose to not provide what is needed. He may well be speaking about God who gives His children the right gifts at the right time. I believe that God wants to bless me richly, and I believe that He could give me all things if it were for the benefit and value of His children. It has taken time for me to see that my will is different than God's will. I have experienced that God gives me everything that I need. Yes, I have wanted more, but I have learned that God delivers to me exactly what I can accept and understand and deal with at the time. When I feel overwhelmed, I am reassured by my experiences that I actually have all that I need to proceed. God extends my limited view without breaking my spirit.

James 2:17-20

Similar to the ideas expressed earlier in the chapter, James now suggests that there is no value for us if we choose to act in faith unless we are also willing to do works that demonstrate our faith. He cites a specific non-example by explaining how the devils have a clear knowledge of who Christ is but are incapable of doing the work of the Savior and simply shudder; they believe that Jesus is the Christ, but they do not show it by their works. Thus, they do not truly have faith that will save.

James 2:21-23

James then provides examples of people, specifically Abraham and Rahab, in the Scriptures who have demonstrated their faith by the work that they did to close the second chapter of his epistle. James describes important characteristics of Abraham in verses 22-24 claiming Abraham's works made his faith perfect and his works were counted toward his righteousness. James also calls Abraham a friend of God. Lastly, James claims the example of Abraham demonstrates how works and faith together justify us before God. Again, he uses expressions like we have a rich understanding of how he is using them, and so we must explore some Old Testament passages to gain more insight. It has always been fascinating to me that much of what we speak is unspoken, as if others understand what we are trying to express in the economy of words we select. Our words are colloquial; thus, our meanings are veiled in time and location. Writing is yet another abstraction of speech, for you cannot hear my voice with its inflection and tone. Add to that the translation from one language to another, and still more can be lost. How then am I truly to grasp the meaning in Scripture being not only separated by time and location but also by language, writing, and translation? I must seek a higher power, one that can understand and break such artificial barriers and constraints. The source is the Spirit of revelation. Although the explanation is circular, the

Scriptures suggest a pattern that can be followed to understand scriptures and messages from God.

1. Hear the word of God spoken and written by His servants.
2. Let the word sink deep into your heart.
3. Have a deep desire in your soul for righteousness.
4. Obediently follow the gospel laws, ordinances, and covenants.
5. Raise your voice in prayer, asking in faith to know the truth.

James has encouraged us to use at least three of these steps as we seek wisdom.

James 2:24-26

James ends this chapter by providing two more examples of his completeness—wholeness—perfection theme. The first is about body and spirit, and the second is about faith and works. Thus by giving a parallelism, James explains that when the spirit leaves the body, we say that the person is dead, and that likewise, when works are gone from our actions, our faith must also be dead. Again, without our spirits being combined with our bodies, the body decomposes, and likewise, without works supporting our faith, our faith will slowly deteriorate.

To summarize, chapter two teaches us that:

1. To be more like our Savior, we must become more whole, mature, and perfect in our actions and evaluations.

2. The royal law is a law of accountability and agency (atonement).

3. Our actions, works, and deeds need to be in alignment with our words, thoughts, and beliefs.

Again, let's pause to think about some of the ideas James presented.

Sorting and Bundling: Integrative Questions for Reflection

What is the difference between respecting people and being a respecter of people?

The Old Testament presents the instructions and we are to determine the lessons, while the New Testament provides the lessons and morals and we are to determine the daily actions. How does this idea suggest a difference between the Law of Moses and the Law of Christ?

What can you do to better understand and live the Law of Christ?

Define conversion. What are the steps of conversion? Is there any particular order to the steps of conversion?

Where are you on the continuum of conversion? What is your next step?

Read the parable of the unmerciful servant Matthew 18:23-35. Have you ever been in a situation where you needed compassion?

Have you ever been able to grant forgiveness and/or compassion to another in need?

What can you do in your life to help you be more likely to be a merciful servant of God?

How can you apply the five-step pattern listed above in your scripture study?

_____

_____

_____

James Chapter Three

James 3:1-2

In chapter three, James returns to his theme of consistency. He begins by briefly explaining that the teacher is held to a different standard than the student and suggests that many of us ought not aspire to the position of teacher. He then immediately teaches us about an important characteristic of God, the ultimate teacher, that He is perfect, speaks perfectly, and therefore able to control the whole body. Peter said, "Christ also suffered for us, leaving us an example, that ye should follow his steps: who did no sin, neither was guile found in his mouth."[48] James and Peter are expressing similar thoughts: Christ is perfect (committed no sin), and He speaks perfectly. But James goes further to explain that because He speaks perfectly, He also can control the whole body.

James 3:3-10

James next uses a series of comparisons, demonstrating how a small thing commands a larger body: bit and horse, rudder and ship, tongue and body. He then chides us for boasting that we can control everything and points out that this belief is unwise. James specifically points out that man is incapable of controlling his tongue (a small member) and then, by implied conclusion, that he is unable to use small things properly to command the larger body, a trait he just told us Christ certainly has. James further points to how man both praises God and curses other men with this same small member, the tongue, and suggests that this ought not be the case. Here again, James points out our partiality. He does not condemn us for not controlling the tongue, but his warning is quite clear that this behavior is not the action of a perfect man.

James 3:11-13

James expands this lesson on partiality by providing two more natural and concrete examples. He reminds us of the operation of fountains that will either produce sweet water or bitter water, but never both. Then he points out that each plant produces its own proper fruit; fig trees do not produce olive berries. It may be said that James has presented a series of parables for us to learn from. Typically this teaching method employs common objects and easily accessible knowledge. To hear the story or lesson is to acknowledge practical information, nothing earth-shattering, and this is certainly the case with the examples James has presented.

The intent of this teaching method, however, is to provide students both the opportunity to interpret a deeper message and for them to develop a personal application of principles taught. Christ taught in parables; by so doing, He conveyed religious truths to His followers who were prepared and inspired to hear His gospel message. Although James's epistle is intended for the tribes of Israel, who should be knowledgeable about the Law of Moses and the need for salvation, not all of its members would have recognized the coming of the Messiah in the corporal form of Jesus Christ; thus, readers of the epistle would know the teaching method while still not understanding that a gospel message was being taught.

James 3:14-18

Throughout chapter three, James provides a series of small parables. His lessons are being taught in a letter, a form that does not allow for dialogue, and so James, not wanting us to miss the lesson, further explains. He concludes that followers of Christ, whose faith is being tried and perfected, should focus on having good conversation and doing good works. Actions such as these will show others the disciples' hopes and personal qualities. Actions such as these are inspired from heaven and will help the disciple on her process of seeking perfection. From the text, we see that the stages of perfection include accepting a purer path, seeing the wisdom of peace and gentleness, developing the qualities of pliancy, meekness, and good intent, and abandoning partiality to seek wholeness and the peace of God.

In summary, chapter three persuades us:

1. Do not become leaders that seek glory and fame of ruling over others, but instead be a disciple who follows a perfect God.

2. Become aware that by changing small elements of our lives we can become less partial and therefore more whole.

3. Perfection is a process whose roots are pure and righteous.

Sorting and Bundling:
Integrative Questions for Reflection

In *Mere Christianity*, C.S. Lewis stated, "Pride gets no pleasure out of having something, only out of having more of it than the next man... It is the comparison that makes you proud: the pleasure of being above the rest. Once the element of competition is gone, pride is gone."[49] How is judging others connected to pride?

What would happen if you tried to stop competing with others (mentally, physically, socially, spiritually)?

Reread James 3:17. List the steps of developing wisdom.

Which characteristics of wisdom do you already possess? Which one can you begin to develop?

What will your first action step be to develop wisdom?

Draw a circle in the space provided (or, maybe on a separate piece of paper), this circle represents all the knowledge in the world. Now draw a line from the

From Straw to Pillar

center of the circle to the outside edge. From this line, create a piece of pie that represents how much of the world's knowledge you actually know, label this *Things I know I know*. Now duplicate your piece of pie and label the next section, *Things I know I do not know*. And now repeat the piece of pie a third time and label this section, *Things I think I know but really don't know*. The fourth section of the circle represents, *Things you don't even know you don't know*. How does this exercise help you understand the difference between what you know and what God knows?

What one thing could you do today to increase what you know?

_____

_____

_____

James Chapter Four

James 4:1-3

The transition between chapters three and four is about peace and war. We move from the idea that righteousness starts with peace to a question about why we fight and have war. The question James presents to us is basically: when we know the steps of Christ's path and we are actively seeking good things, why do bad things happen to us? And his response is simple: because we ask God for the wrong things, we "ask amiss." James says that we are too consumed by our own lusts that we think mostly about ourselves and our needs and our desires. When we focus on ourselves, our attention is partial. God focuses and loves the entire human race; He is whole in His thinking and compassion. In comparison, our partiality derails us from wholly loving our neighbor.

James 4:4-8

James continues to point out the causes of our fighting (both internal and external). He explains that we seek the friendship of the world instead of God's friendship. Then he provides a way for us to overcome our natural selves and receive grace from God—but we must first submit to God and resist the devil. James instructs us to seek God. How? First we cleanse our hands (ye sinners) and purify our hearts (ye double minded). Sounds like we have to clean up outward and inward behaviors, the things we do and the things we feel and/or think. Does this make you think of the "employees must wash their hands" signs you sometimes see in the restroom of a business? Well, we are the employees and must go through the act of washing our hands. But of course that action has much larger implications in the real world; if those employees don't wash their hands and then serve us, customers could become unwell. James gives the reason why we wash: to purify from our double mindedness. The Greek term for double minded is *dipsychs,* or two souls, and the psalms suggest that this refers to a double heart with a proud tongue.[50] So, employees, wash your hands to be able to serve in a healthy way!

James 4:9-11

At first reading, verse 9 sounds fairly dismal: "Be afflicted, and mourn, and weep." But given the entire epistle thus far, James is taking another opportunity to point out that the path to God will mean that we will need to endure trials and that we need to learn humility before receiving the greater blessings of salvation. He wants us to internalize that doers are not judges; disciples are not masters; partiality is not perfection.

James 4:12-17

In the second half of chapter four, James seems to be anticipating questions from the readers of the epistle. It appears that he is responding to questions about the need for humility. For those who are no longer living in the homeland because they have been taken into captivity and/or scattered, humility might be a quality that they think they may already possess, but the issues James raises are not so much about living conditions as they are about attitude. First, James states, there is but one lawgiver and one judge. Clearly God is that lawgiver and judge, and we obviously try to take over His role, usurping power that is not ours when we judge others. Then James criticizes us for claiming that we know how our future will happen. Again, we have usurped power that is not ours but belongs to God. James advises that we should stop trying to be more important than we actually are and to stop trying to control God, telling Him how our lives will go. In contrast, we should instead ask God what His will is for us—and when we know His will, do it!

Chapter four gives simple pieces of advice.

1. To become the friends of God, we must think of others more than we think about ourselves and our lusts.

2. To seek God, we need to cleanse the inner and outer parts of our lives (humble ourselves).

3. To respect God's place as lawgiver and judge, we ought to seek to understand His will for us and become willing to do it.

Sorting and Bundling: Integrative Questions for Reflection

Compare Matthew 6:24 with James 4:4. How can servants become friends of God?

Is there anything in your life that you need to stop doing to be a better friend of God?

What does humility mean to you?

Make a list of people you believe are humble. List other qualities that these people might also have.

What could you do today to be more like one of the people on your humility list?

What actions do you need to take with family members to allow God to be in charge?

How can you learn to ask for the will of God to be done?

_____

_____

_____

James Chapter Five

Chapter five, as the conclusion to James's epistle, rehearses several ideas raised earlier in the letter and then gives final pieces of advice. James follows the example of Moses when he spoke on many occasions to the children of Israel. One of the techniques used by Moses was to rehearse important stories and events that had occurred in the history of the chosen people. By doing this he reminded them of the goodness and mercies of their God and how He had never forgotten them.[51] Here, in the concluding chapter of James's epistle, James not only rehearses past events but prophetically speaks of Christ's second coming. However, "James does not merely pass along tradition. He creatively reshapes and applies tradition."[52] James hopes that his community will regain its chosen identity by following limits of speech, behavior, and relationships. These boundaries, while mirroring statues from the Law of Moses, are given for members of the community to internalize; thus, James preaches the Gospel of Christ.

James 5:1-6

In the first verses, the rich are punished for their misguided actions and allegiances. James points out that they have put their trust in material wealth and further that they lived in wealth even in times of hardship. Verses 2 and 3 echo a part of the Sermon on the Mount where Christ warns that treasures should be laid up in heaven and not earth, because earthly treasures can be corrupted and/or stolen.[53] James even uses similar images of corruption: moth and rust. Interestingly, gold and silver, two elements James mentions, should not rust if they are kept pure and unmixed; the corrosion spoken of is an outward show that the elements are not truly pure. Additionally, the rich have defrauded others in an effort to maintain and keep their supposed wealth, and they have added little to the world through their own work. Lastly, in verse six, the rich are accused of condemning and killing Christ.

Many assume that James is speaking to the wealth of the world, and he certainly is, but it also seems possible that he is talking to the children of Israel as a whole. The people of Israel had received a multitude of blessings, a promised land, and the protection of God in peace and war; they indeed were rich in knowledge and blessings. But Israel misused their blessings and became proud, excluding others and keeping their wealth to themselves. Like the cursed fig tree that was leafy and beautiful from afar but had no fruit to offer, Israel was full of ceremony and show but incapable of offering valuable fruit to others. These richly blessed people should have known more than any other the signs of the Messiah.

Daniel, Hosea, Zechariah, Isaiah, and Jeremiah all speak about the last days, the trials that would occur for the children of Israel and the world, and the second coming of the Messiah. If James had studied Scripture, and it appears he did, he would have been aware of these prophecies. Add to this that James has a particular perspective of being the brother of Jesus Christ, who he has accepted as his Savior and Redeemer. What if James's letter is an attempt to contact the scattered children of Israel, to let them know about the events that had happened in Jerusalem and be encouraged that the actual coming of the Messiah had occurred? Perhaps in their captivity, the lost tribes of Israel have forgotten their true identity and heritage and have forgotten the stories and the traditional education of their children; perhaps they have chosen to follow other gods. James seeks to reconnect with all the scattered and captive, and so he speaks words that he hopes will be heard in their hearts.

James 5:7-8

James once again asks for us to have patience. He uses a common agricultural example about fruit production and how the harvesters wait for both the spring and autumn rains. This is the same patience that the Lord has for all of us, and He is patiently waiting for the times and seasons that have been prophesized by His holy prophets about His second coming. The Lord is waiting and giving all of us time to go through a process of learning and growing, hoping that we choose to follow Him and seek perfection. In these verses, James asks us to believe and establish open hearts that are able to hear truth.

James 5:9-11

James then reminds us about how a community works together, seeking God. He tells us not to have grudges (or judgments against each other), and he asks us to follow the prophets, especially the example of Job. Job is used here not only as an example of a prophet but as a man possessing patience and maybe also to drive home the idea of integrity and wholeness. We can read of Job's integrity in the twenty-sixth and twenty-seventh chapters of the book of Job. Job responds to Bildad's lack of empathy by speaking highly of the greatness and strength of God. Job says:

> How hast thou helped him that is without power? How savest thou the arm that hath no strength? How hast thou counseled him that hath no wisdom? He hath compassed the waters with bounds, until the day and the night come to an end. The pillars of heaven tremble and are astonished at his reproof. Lo, these are parts of his ways: but how little a portion is heard of him? All the while my breath is in me and the spirit of God is in my nostrils; My lips shall not speak wickedness, nor my tongue utter deceit. God forbid that I should justify you: till I die I will not remove mine integrity from me. My righteousness I hold fast.[54]

At the time of this reproof, Job is not in easy circumstances; nevertheless, he refuses to let go of his integrity. Job seems to imply that he already possesses integrity and is unwilling to relinquish it and that, in some way, integrity and righteousness are synonymous. Even in the depth of suffering, Job teaches his friends and, therefore, his community, openly declaring the power of God and his own desire to do God's will. We might interpret that Job has a higher goal than simply completing his life's mission and fulfilling his destiny. Job apparently has experienced some form of greater happiness and seeks now to "see God"[55] in a whole and complete state, a God "who will judge every one of us, sooner or later, according to that Law of right and wrong which He has written on our hearts"[56] and then to be accepted of his Lord. To wait on the Lord, doing His will always, seems to be the desire (and ability) of Job. This is the patience of Job. This should also be the goal of the community, with each member helping the next to aim higher and be more willing to have integrity, to be whole, and to be willing to seek perfection.

Based on James's descriptions thus far in his epistle, the last days are not going to be easy but full of trials and overwhelming for many. I like the following from Max Lucado, who suggested that when faced with an overwhelming task (such as seeking perfection), we should "do what David did. Turn a deaf ear to the old voices. And, as you do, open your eyes to new choices. Others focused on the obvious. David searched for the unusual. Since he did what no one expected, he achieved what no one imagined."[57]

James 5:12-16

James continues to give us tools to creatively solve the problems in our lives. He advises: don't be compelled to swear or make oaths, but simply do what you say you will do, and don't do what you say you won't. In afflictions, pray and sing psalms of gratitude. In sickness, seek support from others, including their prayers and ask for the healing powers of the elders. Repent of your faults. Pray for others. All of these will help a community overcome problems. And while each is simple, each is powerful.

Some of the actions are directed toward God while others are to our fellow beings.

God
- Pray
- Sing psalms
- Repent

Fellows
- Seek others for support
- Seek the elders to heal
- Pray for others

The list begins with actions to take for ourselves; we pray to God, show our gratitude to Him, and repent of our sins. Then the list is repeated: seek others for support sounds a lot like seeking God for support (prayer). Seeking the elders for healing is similar to singing psalms where we recognize and rejoice in the power of God and the blessings He has to offer if we acknowledge Him and ask for help. Praying for others to help, support, and heal them is like the process of repentance wherein we seek the power and love of God to heal and forgive us of errors, to make us whole.

James 5:17-20

James ends his epistle with a reference to a powerful prophet, Elijah. Elijah was but a man, but he was a called servant of God and had the powers of a prophet. Elijah prayed for a drought, and it occurred, and he prayed for the drought to end, and it did. The lesson here is that prayer can be a very powerful tool when it is used to do God's will. Lastly, James encourages us to help others by helping to convert them to the gospel message.

So what brings all these seemingly isolated ideas into coherence? James shows us throughout his epistle that there is a process of perfection. Today this idea has been criticized as unreasonable, and many have changed the process, trying to make other pursuits seem more appealing, easier, and doable. Despite its difficulty, James wants us to seek perfection. He exposes the snares we may encounter and provides us tools to make progress toward gaining integrity and doing the will of God. In summary, these are the messages of chapter five:

1. Do not be deceived by the "rich" of the world.
2. Be patient.
3. Use simple "tools" to relieve pain and suffering.
4. Share with others what is deep in your heart.

James contains many lessons. The lessons have been summarized at the end of each chapter of this book. These summary points are now arranged thematically in the chart below. The first row shows outward actions that we can take and things that we can do. The second row contains inward actions—things to think, understand, and feel. The third row suggests characteristics that we should acquire and things we should become. These three rows represent three levels of commitment: things to do outwardly (public agreements), things to do inwardly (personal commitments), and things to strive to become (godly commitments).

	Chapter One	Chapter Two	Chapter Three	Chapter Four	Chapter Five
Do	(1) There is value in gaining experience, faith, and wisdom through trial (4) Opportunities come when we seek wisdom	(3) Our actions, works, and deeds need to be in alignment with our words, thoughts, and beliefs	(1) Do not become leaders that seek glory and fame of ruling over others, but instead follow a perfect God	(2) To seek God, we need to cleanse the inner and outer parts of our lives (humble ourselves)	(3) Use simple "tools" to relieve pain and suffering (4) Share with others what is deep in your heart
Know/ Feel	(2) We need to know our individual spiritual identities (3) Our earthly missions are important to our salvation	(2) The royal law is a law of accountability and agency	(3) Perfection is a process whose roots are pure and righteous	(3) To respect God's place as lawgiver and judge, we ought to seek to understand His will for us and do it	(1) Do not be deceived by the "rich" of the world
Be	(5) The power of the pure love of Christ can affect our lives	(1) To be more like our Savior, we must become more whole, mature and perfect in our actions and evaluations	(2) Become aware that by changing small elements of our lives we can become less partial and therefore more whole	(1) To become the friends of God, we must think of others more than we think about ourselves and our lusts	(2) Be patient

Investigating the Epistle of James has encouraged an historical approach, a discussion of language and translation, a look at styles of persuasion, a brief exegesis, and a review of many scriptural stories. We have seen that James has been educated in Hebrew Scripture and that, in many ways, he has adopted the rhetoric and speaking style of the great prophets of the Old Testament. James writes to an audience who he assumes is like-minded and trained in Jewish history and patterns. Although he does not explicitly state his sources, options can be identified, mostly from the Old Testament or the lessons of Christ. Reflection on the topics James presents reveal that his message is a reminder that as God's people we must act outwardly and inwardly in ways that demonstrate our acceptance of the covenant of peace[58] He has offered.

Lyn Bair

Sorting and Bundling:
Integrative Questions for Reflection

Think about how impatient the world has become: microwave ovens, streaming news stories, instant messaging, and texting. How can we learn patience in our hurry-up-and-deliver world?

One of the qualifiers for civilization was a separation of duties and roles in the community. Since we are all part of a community, how can we show belief in the members of our community by asking for help?

How can we show support of our community members when we pray for them?

When you approach God in prayer, what are your motives?

What were the blessings of the fathers that Abraham sought?

What must you do to be more able to seek blessings and gifts from heaven?

How can you become more willing to share with God the hidden feelings of your heart?

Lyn Bair

FIRST PRINCIPLE: FAITH

> …what matters in religious experience involves much more than what we believe (or what we do not believe).
>
> —Elaine Pagels[59]

I wonder how the early converts, those who followed the teachings of the resurrected Lord, saw themselves. Were they a group of Jews who recognized the fulfillment of Scripture and accepted that Messiah had come? Were they just a group of people who accepted the ideas that Jesus of Nazareth had taught as true? Christ's teachings were but an oral tradition. It is difficult to remember everything that I have heard that inspired me. Today I can return to books on CD or videos when I want to hear something again. In high school, I learned to take notes during history lectures, but I'm certain I only recorded about 10 percent of what the teacher shared.

For the early Christian converts, I suspect that very few people were actually writing down what was being taught orally. As Christ inspired many during his ministry, I'm certain that I had a teacher or two that gave me new information that was life-changing. I, however, had an advantage over these early converts; I could study other works that had been written on the same topic. How did the early Christians study the words of Christ if they were not written? What did they have available to help make sense of the new applications Jesus was teaching? It seems a small thing now, but I remember when a teacher pointed out to me that the Little Engine That Could was female and that it was natural for her to stop and help. In this case, I returned to the original text to see if she was right. Similarly, to better understand Jesus's oral messages, we can return to the Old Testament text to see if these *new* teachings are true.

The Epistle of James reads more like a speech than a well-formed letter. One way to understand its organization is to see the epistle as a way to review our knowledge of the basic principles of the gospel as taught by the prophets of the Old Testament and fulfilled by Jesus Christ. James reminds us of the basic teachings and provides examples of how these teachings can be enhanced. He chooses to review the principles of faith in salvation, repentance through sacrifice, actions that bring acceptance, and doing the will of God. Remember that James is writing or perhaps speaking to members of the tribes of Israel and that they are already aware of these basic principles. Instead of introducing the concepts for the first time, James is suggesting how these principles are compatible with the new teachings of Jesus Christ. In essence, while some things have changed, the basic beliefs remain stable. James emphasizes that while there are actions that make each principle real for the disciple, the internalization of the principles is a gift from God.

The workshop presenter paused for the audience members to prepare a list of talents. I paused long enough to admit, *this is a daunting task,* and I'm sure that I looked around at the work of other participants before beginning my own list. Psychologically it's easier for me to make a list of what I lack, instead of what I have. One of the items I finally placed on my list was that I could find information I didn't know. When I don't know something, my first recourse is to read on the subject. Reading and studying about a subject gives me the initial confidence to move forward. And once the idea is in my head I seek to find patterns and examples associated with this new information. When we act using our talents, we gain confidence to change. We all have spiritual gifts. These, the scriptures tell us, are for the betterment of the whole community. One of the spiritual gifts that is important to me is to be able to believe in other's words and testimonies. When we act using our spiritual gifts, we gain power to change our lives. After his introduction, James aptly first discusses the principle, the gift and talent of faith.

James's epistle contains 108 verses arranged in five chapters. In the text, the word *faith* occurs in eleven verses (James 1:3, 6; 2: 1, 5, 17, 18, 20, 22, 24, 26; 5:15). From these simple counts of the occurrence of the word *faith,* it seems that if one wanted to study what James knows and can communicate about this concept that the second chapter of his epistle would be the place to start looking.

When we study the chapter two verses, we learn first that James connects faith to the Lord Jesus Christ, and he implies that we are whole in our faith (not partial) when we judge others as God does; thus, if we have faith, we want to emulate the character of God. Second, James teaches that the poor of the world have abundant faith. So we conclude that to develop great faith, we should learn to admire the quality of faith that the poor possess. Third, when works are added to faith, faith becomes alive; when faith and works are united, faith is made whole and perfect. We therefore reason that to have a living and perfect faith, we must also have actions that complement our faith. Let's investigate each of these "faith" lessons further.

Emulation

James's first lesson is that faith is directly connected to the Lord Jesus Christ. Remember that James has studied the Scriptures, and he knows the stories from the Old Testament. Well, there are not too many passages contained in the Old Testament that use the word *faith*; it's more of a New Testament theme. But there is one story where Moses says, "They are a very forward generation, children in whom is no faith."[60] This is said before the children of Israel cross over the Jordan River into the promised land, and Moses takes one last time to rehearse their history and teach them. The text for his message is found in Deuteronomy 32. First, he reminds his people that God is their rock and is perfect because He makes judgments that are just and true (verses 3-4). Then he declares that God is their Father and has ever tended to Israel's needs (verses 6-14). Then he teaches that God, the rock of their salvation, has been lightly esteemed and that Israel has been unmindful and unfaithful toward Him (verses 15-20). Next, Moses prophesizes that Israel will be scattered because of their forgetfulness, pride, and lack of understanding and wisdom with respect to the blessings God had given them (verses 21-29). To drive the point home, Moses then describes the fruit produced by the house of Israel as bitter and poisonous and compares it to the fruit of Sodom and Gomorrah (verses 30-33).

Near the end of the chapter, he reemphasizes the point made in verse 20, where God will hide His face from Israel because their children have "no faith" by instructing that Israel should "set their hearts unto all the words which I testify among you this day" and that they should obey and teach their children, stressing that this counsel is more than vain words but that it represents what is most important in their lives (verses 46-47).

When I get to verses 46 and 47, and read, "It is your life," I want to go back to the beginning of the chapter and really understand what Moses is teaching. As I reread, I feel he is teaching about faith. Similarly, when James teaches about faith in chapter two, he begins just like Moses, connecting faith to God who is perfect and who Moses describes as not partial but whole in His judgment. What is different from the Old Testament lesson is that James now connects faith to the Lord Jesus Christ, our Redeemer, who has the same qualities as the God Moses discourses about in Deuteronomy. Both lessons encourage me to base my life and actions on having faith in my Redeemer. And it seems obvious to me that I must know more about the characteristics of the God I worship.

James's approach and teachings suggest a strong connection to the thirty-second chapter in Deuteronomy, especially about the perfect quality of God's actions and judgments. If I then return to Moses's discourse to gather a broader understanding, I hear him tell me that I need a clear picture of God, who He is, and what great things He has accomplished. Further, I need to know who I am and remember the blessings I have received from God. I need to know that God cares for me just like the mother eagle cares for, coaxes, and teaches her babies to fly (Deuteronomy 32:11). Moses's instruction convinces me that I show my understanding, wisdom, and faith by accepting God as the rock of my salvation. I treasure the words of God and teach them to my children. And finally, I show my gratitude and faith by producing good fruit.

I know from my own experience as a teacher that children only hear small parts of what I say and that they learn more from what they can see demonstrated. And I know that repeated, consistent demonstrations have more power to convince than a single perfect classroom presentation. So I teach children best when my daily actions demonstrate what I already know. The same principle is true about my knowledge of God, and I believe that consistent actions of how I have faith in God or how I am trying to emulate God by not being a respecter of people are similarly demonstrative. Thus, I read into James's (and Moses's) message about faith that I should try to emulate the characteristics of God that I understand and have faith in.

James not only connects our faith to the Lord Jesus Christ, and implies emulation of some character traits, but he also makes the point that unlike human beings, God, in this situation, judges His children perfectly. At the end of Leviticus 19, a chapter that James references often, Moses concludes, "Just balances, just weights, a just ephah, and a just hin, shall ye have."[61] And the book of Deuteronomy describes the types of weights and measures we should have, specifically: "perfect and just weight, a perfect and just measure."[62] Just and perfect, balances and weights, what does this all mean?

Balances are the tools we use to make measurements. If our scales are not leveled, the measurements we make on them will not be accurate or fair. Perfect weights and measures become the standards that are used to compare all measurements against. If these are not just, then the balances will always be inaccurate and tipped too far to one side or the other. Even the specific measures are interesting, for they cover various types of measurement: liquid, dry, and weight.[63] These are the measuring values for sales and trades; in short, these are part of the tools we use to make economical judgments. So it seems that Moses counsels us to be honest in all our dealings with our fellowmen to the same degree that we would monitor the accuracy of our economical transactions, even to a very small degree or weight.

I have two sons. Both were involved in the Cub Scout program, and both raced Pinewood Derby cars. These small cars are precisely measured before the race begins. I was always amazed at the precision scales Scout Leaders used. They were far more accurate than what we were using at home. In eight years of Pinewood Derby races, I learned precisely measured five- ounce cars, with true and friction-conscious wheels were the champions. The effort and attention we pay to such minute details is amazing. I wonder what would happen if we gave similar attention to our daily actions as we do to the weight of a child's racing car?

The message James shares about faith seems clear: to have faith in Christ, faith that allows us to make perfect judgments, we must also use the best tools and the most perfect devices. It is in this way that we will be able to make sound comparisons against perfect measures. Thus, we demonstrate our faith when we are patient enough to wait to make judgments until we have the proper tools and know that our standards are perfect and that we have the perfect tools to do the job of making righteous judgments.

Even if we have the right tools, we still need to know how to use them properly. Access to the right tools does not necessarily guarantee knowledge of the proper use of those tools. So we might ask, if we declare that we have faith in Christ, do we really know what to do with our faith; can we use the tool correctly? Before reading James's answer, spend some time thinking about the tools you have and how you might use them to increase your faith.

Sorting and Bundling:
Integrative Questions for Reflection

What is faith?

If you were asked to talk about an important lesson you have learned, what would you share?

What are your talents?

Read Matthew 25:14-30. What can you do to gain more confidence in your talents?

What spiritual gifts have you been blessed with?

How might you develop one of your spiritual gifts to have power to change your life?

What does it mean to have faith in the Lord Jesus Christ?

What are the characteristics of God? (What makes God, God?)

Read Luke 6:46-49. What do you need to do to lay your foundation on the Rock?

How can your actions better emulate a quality of Jesus?

What areas of your life are you most particular about?

It is important to have the right tools to do any job. How do you employ your discipleship tools?

Create an action plan to better use the tools you have been blessed with. What one thing can you begin today to increase your faith in Christ?

_____

_____

_____

Admiration

James's second lesson about faith is that the poor have rich, abundant faith. Perhaps the first question to ask is who are the poor? Some topical synonyms of *poor* found in the Scriptures include: afflicted, almsgiving, charity, destitute, needy, welfare, and widows. But there are also those that are poor in spirit—the meek. What links these descriptors together are that these people, the poor, are humble and willing to learn, listen, and be obedient. Further, they are the gentle and forgiving of the world. To these, James claims that God gives abundant faith. In response to our previous question about using the tools of faith correctly, James strongly guides us to accept that we must be humble, gentle, and forgiving.

In the Sermon on the Mount, Christ promises the poor the kingdom of heaven. Although we have seen James connect many ideas to the Sermon of the Mount, are there other places in the Scriptures where James could have learned about this principle of the poor being rich in faith and receiving great blessings from the Lord? The answer is yes. The very last chapter of Isaiah begins with: "Thus saith the Lord, The heaven is my throne, and the earth is my footstool: where is the house that ye build unto me? And where is the place of my rest? For all those things hath mine hand made, and all those things have been, saith the Lord: but to this man will I look, even to him that is poor and of a contrite spirit, and trembleth at my word."[64] The chapter begins with the Lord declaring the greatness of His creations in heaven and on earth, and then He proclaims that the most prized creation is a person who is poor, contrite, and giving proper devotion. Isaiah goes on to declare many blessings of comfort and peace, including a new heaven and earth for these righteous people. Thus a combination of this Old Testament passage and statements by Christ at the Sermon on the Mount provide the basis for James's teaching here in his second chapter.

Paul too teaches us about the importance of the poor in his first letter to the Corinthians. After discoursing on the diversity of spiritual gifts that God makes available to us, he talks about the members of the body. I believe he is talking about all the people that are members of the church congregation that come together to create the kingdom of God, and here he says, "Much more those members of the body, which seem to be more feeble, are necessary: and those members of the body, which we think to be less honorable, upon these we bestow more abundant honor."[65] In this passage Paul calls our attention to our actions "we think to be less honorable" and then counters that with the actions of God "upon these we bestow more abundant honor." Basically we do not value or honor those that we consider to be the weak (or poor), but God not only honors them but bestows spiritual gifts abundantly to them.

James has a desire that his readers will admire and want to acquire the great quality and quantity of faith that the poor in spirit possess. It seems that a first step for us is that we understand what types of qualities the poor have and make a decision about whether or not those qualities are worthwhile for us. By presenting the poor as a model of the type of person James believes we should all be, I believe he is encouraging us not only to admire them but to also seek to be like them.

I wonder sometimes if I am part of the poor spoken of by James; at other times, I'm certain I am not. For me, being humble is about my attitude and behavior, about whether I can be gracious in times of heightened accolade or extreme criticism, and about my level of patience in a teaching or a learning situation. I have had many mentors in my life. My mentors had something I didn't have; sometimes it was a skill, sometimes a quality of character, sometimes knowledge. In all cases I came to trust that they had some power that I did not have. They were wiser than me. They had a sense of compassion for me and for my current situation. They were often more interested in my success than I was. I guess you could say that I had faith in my mentors; I believed that they offered an example for living that I might want to follow. I admired them. And in most cases, they each would be very humble about saying they mentored me or even provided an example others would want to follow. In my relationship with each of my mentors, I have noticed the following:

1. I knew parts of their personal story.

2. I found truth in the elements of their story that I knew.

3. I saw a connection between their story and their personal actions.

4. I accepted them as successful, or as a leader, or as an example.

5. I saw purpose in following their path because of the outcomes they had experienced and shared as part of their story.

6. I tried to follow their path, striving for enlightenment and peace.

7. I was blessed with various outcomes like personal growth, joy, happiness, and/or contentment by following their example.

8. I reflected on my journey and shared my new story with others.

When I believe that someone is a good example, a mentor, I look at her qualities and at the results of her actions. If I admire someone enough and choose to follow his example, then I am showing an amount of faith in that person. As a graduate student, I enrolled in a methodology and theory seminar. It was the most difficult written material I had ever been assigned to read and digest. Often it took me hours to understand a single page of art historical theory. In seminar discussions I realized that I was not the only student who was struggling. Some days my professor was so analytical that she might have been the only person in the room that really knew what she was talking about. Well, it probably wasn't that bad, but more than once I left class in total awe of her intelligence, background knowledge, and analytical prowess. Later, while preparing for my comprehensive exam I had an opportunity to work one-on-one with this same professor. The day I showed up for my first appointment, I passed a friend of mine rushing out of this professor's office. My friend seemed emotionally or perhaps academically crushed. *What have I gotten myself into*, I thought. *Will I be theorized and analyzed to tears too?* What I discovered in my personal meetings with this professor was how interested she was in helping me pull all the pieces I had studied together. This amazing and brilliant professor was gentle and continued to encourage me to keep reading and studying. She was patient when she disagreed with my conclusions. She was willing to talk through ideas and about pieces of art and kept apologizing for what she didn't know; so she was humble too! I really wanted to be more like her!

I think James would strongly guide us to consider many different aspects of a person: the person's humility, gentleness, and ability to forgive. It is in seeking these characteristics in others, where we would be admiring and following the example of the poor that he refers to in his epistle.

Lyn Bair

Sorting and Bundling: Integrative Questions for Reflection

Read 1 Corinthians 12:1-13:13. List the gifts of the spirit. List the qualities of charity.

To how many *communities* do you belong? (work, church, social groups…)

What is the role of community in your life?

If you are a member of a spiritual congregation, how and why is that important to you?

What are the qualities that God honors and values in His children?

Think about how you spent your day. Create a list of things you did. Try to associate the amount of time spent on each activity during your day. Based on this list, what do you value?

How does God's list of important qualities compare to the list of values your life demonstrates?

Write an action step that would help you bring your values more in-line with what God honors and values.

How can you be more than just an admirer of humility, gentleness, and forgiveness?

_____

_____

_____

Reasoned Conviction

James's third lesson is about faith and works. James attempts to convince us that our expressed faith is made perfect and whole when works are also present and when our works demonstrate our proclaimed faith.[66]

Toward the conclusion of His Sermon on the Mount, Christ warns us to beware of false prophets, and He instructs us how to recognize the goodness of people by the fruit they bear. He gives examples of figs and grapes. The examples of figs and fig trees (sycamores) in the Scriptures are interesting.[67] There is, for example, a passage in 2 Kings about King Hezekiah and the Prophet Isaiah where figs are used to create a healing tool. Isaiah also refers to a variety of fig tree when he talks about the pride of Ephraim, who upon recognizing that the temple in Jerusalem is destroyed, boastfully announces they will produce hewn stones instead of bricks and cedars instead of sycamore to repair the temple.

From these examples, it seems that figs are used to symbolize positive traits—goodness, healing, and excellent quality. But what do figs have to do with faith? The answer may come from combining three New Testament stories: the first, Christ cursing the fig tree, and the second, the parable of the fig tree, and the third, the parable of the vineyard.

In the Gospel of Mark, Christ curses a fig tree for not having fruit when He is hungry. Christ, in company with His apostles, sees the leaves of a fig tree afar off, but upon reaching the tree, the group finds no fruit. Christ then curses the tree. In the Gospel of Matthew,

Christ refers to the parable of the fig tree, saying that when we see fig leaves summer is not far off. And in the Gospel of Luke, another fig tree parable talks about actions to help a fig tree that has yet to produce fruit.

These three gospel references to fig trees offer three symbols about faith. The Luke parable talks about a barren fig tree. When the master of the vineyard wants to cut it down, the servant offers to dig round it and provide rich nutrients (dung) to see if the tree can be helped. "In the Old Testament, the fig tree was a symbol of God's blessings and special love for God's people."[68] Thus when the tree is helped and nourished, this is God intervening and helping the barren tree produce something good. If we represent the tree, then we exhibit faith and do what we can, believing God will intervene if necessary to help us achieve.

The parable from Matthew uses the leafy fig tree as a symbol of time; summer is not far away. Trees respond to the seasons and produce in predictable patterns. In the case of the fig tree, it is lush and leafy prior to summer. Thus we can predict from the signs of nature. Again, if we represent the tree, then we develop in predictable patterns, and one sign precedes the next; our faith generally precedes miracles.

In the cursed fig tree story, from the Gospel of Mark, it is important to know that the fruit of a fig tree develops and ripens before the tree is covered with leaves. Thus, when a fig tree is lush and leafy (as was the case with the fig tree Christ cursed), one could naturally assume the tree would also have fruit to offer. If the fig tree were a human being, we would see all the signs of righteousness, and their appearance would be inviting, but upon closer examination, we would find that they did not really have anything to offer. Perhaps then we can understand Christ's warning us if we are not pure and present the same appearance and offerings, we too may be cursed for our hypocrisy. And just as the cursed fig tree withered the following day, our true intentions will be shown for their real value.[69]

In the language of James, our faith should be the same as our works. Without stating all the references, James draws the conclusion for us: we need more than appearance (outward shows of faith); we need to produce something good (righteous works).

My faith drives me to want to make good choices. It encourages me to continue to follow the path I believe Christ demonstrated and produce "good fruit." My faith urges me to read the Scriptures and to make sense of the stories there. My faith helps me in how I respect myself, how I treat myself, and the self-talk I produce. Sometimes I act as if I have forgotten that my faith is grounded in a belief of a Savior and that I am a child of God; thus, my outward faith may not always appear strong. Times like these make me believe that faith needs to be encouraged on and on and is not a one-shot deal but something to be built and cultivated. My personal experience is one thing, but for you to come to the same reasoned conviction as James, perhaps more ideas to consider are needed.

Elsewhere in the New Testament, Paul offers another explanation of faith. He says, "Faith is the substance of things hoped for, and the evidence of things not seen."⁷⁰ This is the same definition Dante gives to Peter when he is questioned about his faith in the "Divine Comedy." When asked to explain how faith is both a substance and an evidence, Dante responds:

> The deep things that on me bestow
> Their image here, are hid from sight below,
> So that their being lies in faith alone,
> And on that faith the highest hope is founded;
> And thus it is that faith is called a substance.
> And it is from faith that we must reason,
> Deducing what we can from syllogisms
> Without our being able to see more:
> Thus faith is also called an evidence.⁷¹

Dante believes all gifts from God⁷² are not necessarily perceived by the senses; thus they are hidden from man's intellect. The recipient of these spiritual gifts must rely on faith, which becomes the substance of his belief that the gifts exist. Then Dante explains when we reason, we base our conclusions on evidences (generally our proof is tied to our senses or our intellect). When we reason eternal truths, we base our conclusions on evidences of faith. Thus faith is both substance and evidence.

Do we ever take the time, like Dante, to reflect on why we hold certain beliefs? Such reflection allows us to validate and strengthen our beliefs or to reject them as untruths. In this reflective process, there are some basic steps to take, the first of which is to become aware of the beliefs that we hold. Writing these beliefs down can help us verbalize not only the general idea but also some specific elements of the beliefs. After we have written these belief statements, the next step in our reflective process is to determine when and where we first accepted this belief. There is likely a story or a sequence of events that will help us remember the beginnings of each belief statement.

I used to play a game called Tip-it. A plastic tripod balanced with three posts held a tall rod, and at the top of the rod, a small toy man balanced by his nose. To start the game, primary-colored disks were placed equally on the three posts. Using a forked spatula tool, players took turns removing a specific colored disk. Players anxiously waited for their turns hoping they could collect the right needed disk without knocking Tip-it off his perch.

During high school I discovered that writing an expository essay was a little like the game of Tip-it. Getting all the rules right and balancing all the parts and pieces was hard. Fortunately I was not alone (misery really does love company). Near the beginning of my sophomore year, I was assigned to read *Moby Dick*. During the class we discussed the story, characters, and various ideas presented by the author. At the conclusion of our discussions, we would write an essay. Everything was going well, until my essay was returned. Tip-it crashed! I began to hold on to the belief I would never pass English 10. I was always behind in my reading assignments and my writing was very weak. It took many help sessions with my English teacher before I thought about revising my belief. Then one day my teacher asked, "You're good at math, right?" "Yeah" I responded. "Okay, then don't write me an essay. Write me a geometric proof. Here are your givens and here is what you need to prove."

It took 99 steps to solve the problem. And then my English teacher showed me how to move from my proof to write an expository essay that made sense and solved the assigned question. Writing essays in this way opened a new door and allowed me to rewrite a belief about my abilities. Instead of seeing myself as inferior, I learned that effort makes a difference in my success to learn and demonstrate what I know.

The words of our mentors might confirm our personal belief statements. But consider, do the words of God and other inspired leaders confirm our belief statements? When our belief statements put us down, we judge ourselves unfairly, and not as our mentors or leaders or God see us. These statements are not true. When our statements, therefore, are negative with regards to our personal characteristics, we might need to ask, how might we rewrite our belief statements by showing a stronger connection to true principles? The next step, then, may take some time, but it is important to identify evidences in our life and the lives of others that validate each belief statement. It is possible that some statements will have no evidence or perhaps that the evidence will appear thin and without much merit. The realization that our statements have different levels and qualities of evidence will encourage us to compare the belief statements against truth.

Now that we believe that our statements are aligned to true principles and they measure-up to noted and admired experts, then we need to create a plan of action. Our plans should be designed so that the things we do openly show our commitment to our belief statements; what we do must prove to others what we believe.

Here is a quick list of the reflective process to refine our personal statement of beliefs:

1. Write out your belief statements.

2. Determine who or what taught you to think this way.

3. List evidences that support and/or refute your beliefs.

4. If evidence is weak or limited, rewrite beliefs based in truth.

5. Plan action steps that demonstrate your beliefs.[73]

I work in public education; it is a calling. Often the students ask me why I teach. I think I make a difference, maybe not for every child, but for enough that I continue to want to do the job. In 1999, after the school shooting at Columbine High School in Colorado, I felt inspired to write a statement of beliefs for my own high school students. My students were expressing doubts about their future, and they wondered about the value of what they were being taught and how they were spending their time. In response, I simply listed the things I believed in and had a desire to stand for, hoping to inspire my students to express their fears as well as their dreams. I have put my list of beliefs through the reflective process discussed, and I continue to find value in sharing this list with my students and peers.

My statements of belief remind me that I can lead a spiritual life every day. My beliefs certainly affect others, and yet my beliefs harm no one. The work I choose to do is both in line with my professed faith and allows me the opportunity to produce good works. "There is sometimes a tendency to think of a spiritual life as primarily introspective, divorced from the concerns of everyday life and society. This, I believe, is plainly wrong and is also rejected in this epistle. Faith that does not translate into action is no faith at all."[74] This is the reasoned conviction James wants us to see. "An enlightened faith seems very ordinary. One might scarcely notice it. It accepts the way things are and finds God vibrantly present in the most insignificant situations."[75] Our challenge then is to be consistent, to be alert to ordinary signs, and to have our faith and work express the same message.

Are you ready to draft a personal statement of beliefs? Let's review some ideas and then get started.

Lyn Bair

Sorting and Bundling:
Integrative Questions for Reflection

What do you learn from the following references: Genesis 3:7; Micah 4:4; Matthew 7:16; and Revelation 6:13?

Compare yourself with a fig tree. What type of figs are you producing?

What does your faith in Christ lead you to do?

What general beliefs do you have about yourself?

What would your friends say you believe in?

Pick one belief. When did you begin to hang on to this idea?

Referring to your belief above, can you identify events in your life that have confirmed this belief?

Again, referring to the above belief, who else believes as you do?

How can you act on your belief (be a healthy fig tree)?

Write your personal statement of belief. You might want to begin with, *I believe...* or perhaps, _____ *is important to me because...*

_____

_____

_____

Faith and Prayer

If chapter two allows us to understand James's stand with regard to emulation, admiration, and reasoned conviction, chapters one and five provide insight into the benefits of trying your faith and the power personal conversations with God, prayer, can have.

Many people believe in a power greater than themselves, and they work hard to put action toward that belief. They practice and participate in rituals, and they learn new lessons all in an effort to see if their belief has merit. In essence they are testing different principles to see if they are valid for them; they are trying their faith. When they have positive experiences related to these tests, their belief is increased, and they accept more and perhaps even have a desire to test further. This is a method of reaching a reasoned conviction.

As humans we learned about testing our limits very early; we did it as children with our parents. What could we get away with? What was unacceptable? We learned limits, and we learned how our parents would respond to our actions and decisions. Often we reacted badly to new limits. Even years later, people return to these poor reactions as a means of survival. One of the things to do when we are trapped in our own bad habits is to change our patterns of thinking before we act (or react). I suppose the same thing is true when we are not maturing spiritually; we get stuck in our own thinking and cannot act appropriately, or we react without thinking much at all. We become the fig tree that cannot produce fruit.

My mother had a dear friend. She was very involved in the community, at church and with her own family.

From Straw to Pillar

As I grew, she played many roles beyond *friend of my mother*. She provided advice on dozens of topics and in many situations. Perhaps the most important thing I remember her saying was, "Remember who you are and what you represent." Whenever I thought to push my parents' limits, I heard her voice and that phrase. Just as poor habits can develop, so too can we develop positive reactions to events. I have wondered about whether this sweet woman just wanted me be to be good, or was she sharing a deeper message? As a teenager, I settled on the understanding: she just wants me to do the stuff I've been taught at church. As I went to college, I started to see everything I choose to do was connected to lots of other people well beyond my vision, so I better be careful and choose well. When our daughter was born, this little phrase seemed to encourage me to continue to grow and improve and never tire of developing my talents. After the passing of my mother, these words brought compassionate hope, reminding me to search deeper in my own heart for love, acceptance, and understanding.

Like our understanding of a simple phrase, faith at first requires us to test and experience, but at some point in our maturity or faith growth, we need to move from testing everything to accepting some things as true and worth doing all the time. Faith begins similarly to how we test our parents' limits of our own behavior. We try something, and if the response is good, we condition ourselves to do those actions again. If the response is negative, we either try again for a different response, or we try something different.

James tells us trying our faith works patience. I think when most of us test different limits and reactions, we are honestly trying to experience positivity in our lives. In the school business, there are several required standardized tests. Some assess our knowledge of content, others our acquired skills, and still others our interests. Not everyone is good at these tests, and many need coaching to get through the experience. Test-prep companies teach their students to recognize patterns: patterns in questions and patterns in answers. Ultimately the highest scores are earned by getting the greatest number of questions answered correctly. So these companies give their students different tools to answer each type of question. When the answer is not obvious, often a guess-and-check method is employed, which is a little like working the problem backward and hoping the right answer is the first one you pick. If you don't pick well, the method can take too much time, but it's often better than not answering the question at all.

Sometimes we use the same method with issues that relate to our faith; we guess and check, test the result, and decide whether we have the right answer or if we still need to work the problem again. Ultimately this method takes time and gives us a chance to develop patience. As we try our faith, we are testing and working through problems, hoping that the belief system we have in place will be adequate to solve our current issues. If we are successful, we gain confidence. If we fail, our confidence is damaged a little, and we are forced to make a new decision to give the issue more time or to solve it with different means. It is when things do not go smoothly that our faith is really tried, and we are faced with making a decision to continue to believe or to abandon our hope. Through this process, if we continue to believe, our faith will mature, and we will come to learn about God's love, kindness, and His will more and more.

James's other point about faith is that it is connected to prayer and that prayer has power. To be honest, I don't much think about whether or not there are any benefits to prayer anymore; I know that it has worked for me previously, and so I accept its merits. My prayers have been tried, and I have developed patience. For me, the act of praying now seems to be about the quality of my interactions. I pray for a variety of reasons and have great faith that there will be a response and associated feelings. I tend to share my comings and goings with God. I ask for help, and I try to express my gratitude for the blessings I receive. Sometimes I pray just to acknowledge my gratitude. Often I am begging for support.

My daily devotional time doesn't look like what I learned in Sunday school, but it is consistent and is helping me expand my understanding of God's will and how I can best serve Him, helping to accomplish His work in this world. My communication with God is not isolated to morning and night but occurs frequently. It happens when I plan the day, when I drive, and while I'm at work; it happens when I am journaling, and when I am reading and trying to make sense of ideas and situations. It happens when I talk to my children, and it happens when I am quiet and peaceful. Don't think that my life is always perfect; it's not.

Despite setting time aside daily to seek inspiration, I can still paralyze myself by imagining scenarios that cause me great fear. In these moments I find that a formal on-my-knees prayer, coupled with quiet moments to listen for the response of a loving God, gives me both relief and great hope.

I'm not sure which prayer activities show greater faith, and I'm not sure that any really do, or perhaps they all do. Both the "daily" and the "emergency" methods offer me a way to train my mind. The first is a consistent daily practice where I am developing greater understanding and a conscious contact with a loving God. The second is an emergency 911 call where I am in a bind and need help now to calm down and refocus. What I have learned is that both methods have the power to heal me and help me move forward in my life.

James encourages us to ask God specifically for two things: wisdom and healing the sick. It is interesting that one is to heal the mind and the other is to heal the body. In other words, we can ask God to help our insides and outsides, to heal our minds and bodies, to increase our understanding and strength, and to make us whole and perfect.

I think about times in my life when I needed this kind of healing, both body and mind, and it seems that it happens when fear gets the best of me, and my faith wavers. Thus, I understand why James expresses all these ideas together as he teaches about faith. Typically I am a fairly cautious person, and I have great fear about new situations and new people. In my life I have experienced only a few close friendships. I tend not to trust most people until some event helps me see other-

From Straw to Pillar

wise. I suppose I try my friendships and relationships, and instead of developing patience, I develop trust.

Recently I took a new job. I had been asked by my boss to make some fairly drastic changes. I was in a position where everyone looked to me to solve every problem, answer every question, etc. My opinion of my skills was tested. Often I felt very alone and very ineffective. I thought about what to do, but often my insecurities got the better of me, and I was afraid, often paralyzed without the belief that I even knew or had any positive abilities to do the job well. People were talking behind my back, and people were judging me.

Anyway, the transition was not going well, and my faith was shaken. In a dark moment, I reached out to a friend for spiritual direction and help. I walked and ranted and talked—and I finally realized that the problem was inside me, and I needed serious healing of both body and mind. In this particular case, I acted on the promise James offers in chapter five to use the power of prayer to heal. At first I just went through the motions. I thought, *Maybe I'm being more superstitious than faithful, but hopefully these repeated actions will eventually prove to become faithful actions.* Some might call my actions blind faith, but I don't think so; maybe it was a little dark where I found myself, but this has not always been the case. I have experienced the blessings before, and so, although it may be dark now, I am not blind, and I choose to find light, so I move forward into the present unknown, hoping such movement will offer relief.

My experience shows me that Christ offers me relief when I ask with faith to be healed. Paul exclaimed that

Christ is the author and finisher of our faith/salvation.[76] Salvation is a noun and begins with the root verb "to save." To be saved is to be rescued or to be protected from bad results. Lifeguards may save people who are drowning in the water. Friends may save us a place in line (where we avoid the negative result of not getting in to see a show or missing out on something that may be sold out before we get to the front of the line). Christ has authored how we are to be saved in life. He clearly knows how the story goes, but since He is also the finisher, then He had an important and pivotal role of the story. Because of my faith in Christ, I believe that what I do makes a difference for not only me but that I also affect others by my thoughts, actions, and priorities.[77]

Since I accept Christ as my Redeemer, I see purpose in seeking perfection and trying to limit my attachment to temporary earthly wealth and power. Through His atonement, Christ saved me from a life with little purpose, and He helps me know that life is precious. Because I choose to follow the Savior's example, I want to learn what God's will is and follow His will and direction more often. Faith is the first principle of the gospel; it gets everything moving toward a greater belief in a loving God. Faith, according to James, has power to enlighten our minds and heal our diseases. Faith in Jesus Christ encourages us to emulate, adore, and seek for reasoned conviction about our beliefs. Faith is our entrance to greater and deeper understandings and feelings about ourselves and our purpose in this life.

Sorting and Bundling: Integrative Questions for Reflection

How have you tested your limits with family and friends?

If you were asked to describe your faith to a non-Christian, what would you say?

Would your description of faith change if you were talking to a spiritual leader?

How do you communicate with God?

If you have a daily devotional, describe what you typically do. If not, what would you like to start doing?

Do you have *insides* that need to be healed; in what ways would you like your mind enlightened?

Do you have *outsides* that need healing; what disease(s) do you need removed?

What does salvation mean to you?

Lyn Bair

SEEKING LIGHT AND TRUTH

> When the past no longer casts light upon the future; our minds advance in darkness.
>
> —Alexis de Tocqueville[78]

My academic training is in art history, a field where we look at evidence and often attempt to expose intention and meanings. I was taught, therefore, to ask questions of a work of art, trying to identify sources of the artist's imagination and style of execution. I was vigilant of how the artist dealt with issues of contemporary religion, scholarship, and current conventions of artistic expectations yet remained curious as to how the artist would "speak" his own truths, act on his intuition, and display a new invention via his personal style. I desire to apply this training as I read the Epistle of James.

At the very beginning of his epistle, James offers a greeting and then extends an invitation that tests the commitment of his believing readers: become whole.[79] "The opening of the main body of James is clearly significant for the remaining text, and…provides a framework in which to place the more enigmatic content of the epistle."[80] The first twelve verses of the chapter establish the purpose of his epistle, which is introducing all of his ideas that will receive supporting details in the next four chapters. After stating that believers will be tested, James uses the next verses to briefly explain how his readers can achieve the challenge of being whole and perfect. James instructs that this pursuit has two necessary elements: light and truth. To explain the first, he will teach us to seek wisdom; for the second, he will teach us that we must love all people.[81]

Light: James Deals with Contemporary Religion and Scholarship

To understand how light is used in the Scriptures, let us begin with one of the opening verses of the Old Testament: "God said, let there be light: and there was light. And God saw the light, that it was good."[82] Creating (willing, allowing) light is God's first act of creation. This light, which is different than the radiating light of the sun since it was not yet created, dispels the darkness upon God's command.

Many of the references to light in the Old Testament address the physical property of light: lamplight, oil to burn light, or morning light. Some references use light as an adjective; thus we see references to not taking things lightly or insignificantly, such as our esteem for parents. And often we see light being used to mean gentle or soft, as in dew or rain falling.

Isaiah uses the phrase, "Let us walk in the light of the Lord,"[83] addressing a spiritual property of light. Walking in the light of the Lord suggests that we need to follow either God's path or to be under the influence of God or to be in His presence.

The book of Daniel provides instruction about light as well in the story when Daniel interprets Nebuchadnezzar's dream. Remember that the king has had a troubling dream and seeks the interpretation from his wise men (Chaldeans) but will not reveal to them what happened in the dream. He says, "The thing is gone from me."[84] When the wise men are unsuccessful, the king issues a decree that all of them should be killed. Daniel, who would have been considered one of the wise men of the kingdom, shows us a five-step pattern that any of us could follow when we need to understand something:

1. He asks for time to study.
2. He gets together with companions who are like-minded.
3. He prays for wisdom.
4. He waits patiently to receive wisdom and understanding.
5. He expresses gratitude to God.

Ultimately, Daniel is blessed to know the dream and the interpretation. He gratefully says, "Blessed be the name of God…he giveth wisdom…and knowledge… He revealeth the deep and secret things…the light dwelleth with him."[85] It is with this last expression that light dwells with God that seems new or different. If Daniel's gratitude is viewed as a chiasm, then light is equated with wisdom; thus wisdom dwells with God.

The Bible also shows us that descendants or successors are often called lamps or lights. So, "to raise up a lamp to a person signifies his having a posterity to continue his name and family."[86] Thus, to be a father of lights, one would have a great posterity. And when we apply the principle to God, He is the father of a great posterity and therefore the Father of lights. When God renewed His covenant with Isaac, He said, "I will perform the oath which I sware unto Abraham thy father; and I will make thy seed to multiply as the stars of heaven."[87] Following the pattern discussed above, when talking about posterity or seed, God compares Isaac's descendants to the stars and the lights of heaven that are without number, and Isaac becomes a father of lights.

The Apostle John discusses both physical and spiritual concepts of light in his gospel book and in his epistles. He states, "In him was life; and the life was the light of men"[88] and further explains, "God hath given to us eternal life, and this life is in his Son."[89] John here lays out the idea that Christ offers the hope of eternal life to man and that this is the light we seek, and further, this light (eternal life) is to be found in Christ. Thus light in this usage defines a characteristic or power that God possesses that He is willing to give to us through His Son. John's usage of light expands very quickly in his gospel message, and he begins to use the term as a proper pronoun to speak about the Savior. At one point John uses both the verb and pronoun in the same verse, explaining that Christ "was the true Light, which lighteth every man."[90] From this verse we learn that "the true Light," or Christ, provides the power of light or eternal life to all men.

In the gospel of John, the first chapter has a chiasm that turns between verses ten and eleven, which would suggest that verses nine and twelve are giving the same message. Thus we compare "the true Light, which lighteth every man" with "to them gave he power to become the sons of God." By reading the two verses, framed by chiasm, together, we hope to understand them both more perfectly. This reading confirms the idea that the Light is Christ and the light is a power, but it suggests that what lights every man is the hope of becoming the "son of God." Hoping for eternal life seems to be equated with becoming a Son of God.

Peter uses light to suggest another meaning. He says, "But ye are a chosen generation, a royal priesthood, an holy nation, a peculiar people; that ye should shew forth the praises of him who hath called you out of darkness into his marvelous light" (1 Peter 2:9). In Peter's discourse he reminds us who and what we really are (chosen, royal, holy, and peculiar) by greeting us with a variety of titles. He then reminds us that God has introduced us into light. Peter seems to talk about darkness and light as gradations of intelligence and opportunity.

I used to play field hockey. My play had gradations of intelligence and opportunity; sometimes I had a great game. One of my coaches appeared to be a commanding woman, and although I never heard her yell at anyone in anger, when I played less than sterling, there was little doubt about how she felt. She had a matter-of-fact way of giving instructions, and as a matter of fact, that's how she gave compliments too! I remember one day when she was teaching me to *flick* the field hockey ball. She wanted it straighter, stronger, and in an exact place. She stood about fifteen feet in front of me and instructed me to flick the ball down the field. No problem, just not great. Then she told me to flick the ball down the field again, this time through her straddled legs. I gave a painful look of doubt. She insisted. Then I confirmed my doubt by planting the ball solidly into her thigh. She reached down, picked up the ball, and threw it back to me. "Do it again," she instructed. A second flick into her leg, but she was determined that I was going to learn this skill, so we did it again. Finally I flicked the ball between her legs. I'll never forget her next words, "Good job. Now, never forget how much I trust you." I never questioned her trust in me again. She had lit confidence and power, and I never wanted to give her less than my very best. I think having this trust was a lot like being given light from God. He teaches what we need: shows us the Light and gives us His trust: endows us with power. With the light and power, we can accomplish amazing things.

The Bible authors use the term *light* to suggest many things, including a physical property, a power, a verb, an adjective of quantity, as a synonym for eternal life, as a title of Christ, to describe the gift of wisdom and understanding given from God our Father, to indicate the wealth of one's posterity, and to talk about intelligence and opportunity. In his epistle, James states that all good gifts come from the "Father of Light,"[91] which seems to connect to what Daniel expressed, but of course the idea is embedded with an understanding of posterity like Abraham, Isaac, and Jacob. When he uses this title, James adds a clarifying comment that with God, there is no variableness; He doesn't change. Remember that James earlier invited all of us to seek wisdom but cautioned us not to waver. Thus James compares a quality of humans with a quality of God; we waver, but God is unchanging. Why not, then, see that the gifts the Father of Light offers to those wavering souls as wisdom, a good and "perfect gift"?

When James calls the gifts good, I believe he expresses the feelings of the psalmist that the Lord shall give that which is good, meaning "surely his salvation."[92] This connects James's use of light to the ideas expressed by the Apostle John, in that eternal life is somehow connected to light. I am fascinated by James's use of "perfect" when he describes work (verse 4) and gifts (verse 17). When he adds, "That ye may be perfect and entire, wanting nothing," it makes me think that he is really talking about salvation and eternal life. This journey, as described by James, starts with faith and is enhanced by lessons (trials) and made perfect as we gain the gift of wisdom from the Father of Lights. Before turning to the second method that James offers for us to become perfect and to seek truth, let us pause and reflect.

Lyn Bair

Sorting and Bundling:
Integrative Questions for Reflection

Read Isaiah 2:1-5. What does the prophet teach us about walking in the light of God?

Greater understanding takes time and study. What are the advantages of seeking conversation with like-minded people when we seek to increase our understanding?

Compose a gratitude list. List everything you recognize as a blessing.

What is the Light of Christ?

What do we need to do to show more trust in God?

_____

_____

_____

Truth: James Addresses Current Conventions of Thought

The word *truth* is used often, and yet giving a simple definition is difficult. "On the surface it seems a simple concept. But mature reflection and an attempt at defining it invariably leads to the realization that in its full implications it is complex."[93] James uses the actual word *truth* only three times in his epistle, but he refers to the concept throughout his letter, particularly in chapters two and five. At first he says, after introducing the idea that the Father of Lights provides spiritual gifts, "of His own will begat He us with the word of truth."[94] In one reading we could say that the Father of Lights created (begat) us through the word of truth, meaning some ability, or characteristic, or power, or perhaps it is all three of these ideas together. In a second reading, one might suggest that the Father created us and gave us the gift of truth. In another reference, James cautions us not to lie against truth,[95] suggesting that truth is a title. And at the end of his epistle, he equates our mistakes with erring against truth. In these instances, James refers to truth as a power of God, the ideal standard of judgment and something that man has knowledge of and should compare his actions against. I believe in each case, James is using truth to refer to Jesus Christ, much like the Apostle John used "the word" to talk of Christ.

The 85th Psalm provides another clue as to the nature of truth through a series of comparisons. The structure of the psalm uses two chiasms: the first in verses 1 through 6 and the second in verses 8 through 13, with the theme being presented between the two, specifically, salvation. It is in the second structure that we are interested.

v. 8:Lord speaks peace	Saints should not reject God
v. 13:Righteousness	the way follows His steps
v. 9:salvation	glory exists in our land
v. 12:Lord gives what is good	our land's yield increase
v. 10:Righteousness and peace	Mercy and truth
v. 11:Righteousness from heaven	Truth from the earth

By breaking down the structure of the psalm into this double column, I begin to understand that the Lord speaks peace and righteousness, He provides salvation from heaven, and saints should accept God's gifts and follow His path to receive the blessings of mercy and truth while on the earth. The psalmist is explaining that God speaks to His holy prophets and that they in turn write the inspired words for His children on earth. "The Lord will speak"...and "truth shall spring out of the earth," thus Scripture, a physical (earthly) work, has a spiritual (heavenly) source and is true.

 The psalmist also seems to connect truth with righteousness while matching mercy with peace. Therefore, we presume that on earth, we show our acceptance of heavenly truths through our righteous actions while showing our acceptance of heavenly mercy through the peace that we produce. James must have liked the eighty-fifth Psalm for its praise of both light and truth, and he used it as a basis for explaining how these principles might help us on our road to perfection.

In Paul's letter to the Philippians, he talks about being confident, sincere, and "filled with the fruits of righteousness."[96] He reminds us to be mindful of our conversation and to remain humble as we serve God and represent his light. Then he offers, "whatsoever things are true, whatsoever things are honest, whatsoever things are just, whatsoever things are pure, whatsoever things are lovely, whatsoever things are of good report; if there be any virtue, and if there be any praise, think on these things."[97] Paul is teaching us to connect truth with righteousness just as the Psalmist did. And using his repetitive style he explains truth as being honest, just, pure, lovely, and of good report.

I met a young woman who was visiting the Aspen Musical Festival and was impressed by her love of truth. She was very observant and ultra sensitive to the beauty of the world around her. She firmly believed that some things were just right. She also believed that we should do the right things for the right reasons. Often we do the right things, but for wrong motives, for example, we offer help to an elderly lady but we really seek a financial reward for our service. Other times we do the wrong things for the right reasons, for example, we choose *not* to help an elderly woman because we know our real intention to is seek pay for helping. What this young woman taught me was that neither of these situations is right, helpful, friendly, personally positive, or true. William George Jordan stated this lesson in this way: "Truth is the rock foundation of every character. It is the loyalty to the right as we see it; it is courageous living of our lives in harmony with our ideals; it is always—power."[98]

Sorting and Bundling:
Integrative Questions for Reflection

Define truth.

Read Psalm 51. Compare the things David pleads for with what he acknowledges that God truly wants. If you seek God's truth and wisdom, what might God require from you? (Psalm 51:17)

Is repentance connected to truth? Why or why not?

Read Hosea 4:1-6. Hosea claims that there is no truth in the land. Make a list of all the things Israel is doing against truth.

Using the list above, create a list of things you can do to increase your knowledge of God.

_____

_____

_____

Light and Truth: James's Innovation and Enlightened Expression

It is not enough to discuss the symbolic meanings of light and truth separately, for James connects the two and directs us to seek both if we intend to become perfect. James would have been familiar with the connection of light and truth as a phrase found in the Hebrew Bible as "urim and thummim."[99] The Hebrew words, both plural, mean lights and perfections. Jewish sources explain that the urim and thummim were ocular gems worn by the high priest to discern God's will.

John connects light and truth when he states, "But he that doeth truth cometh to the light, that his deeds may be made manifest, that they are wrought of God."[100] The concepts of light and truth here teach that when we act in truth, what we do shows our direct connection to the light of God.

James wants his readers to act in this type of truth. And since he knows what the light of God is, he clearly hopes that his readers will be able to discern God's will for themselves: "If any lack...wisdom, let him ask of God." For James, there is hope, then, that if we follow the principles taught in his epistle, we will be able to seek both wisdom (lights) and act in truth (perfections). James knew that the Hebrew high priests received discernment (wisdom and light) for the children of Israel to direct their actions (of truth and perfection). But he must also believe that we individually can achieve personal discernment by seeking wisdom and truth and light and perfection, even if we can only receive such guidance for ourselves to direct our own individual behavior. He clearly invites "any of you that lack wisdom" to follow his guidance.

My father graduated from Yale University, and so, growing up, I was surrounded by the colors, mascot, symbols, and motto associated with that university. My exposure to these symbols is not, however, universal, so perhaps a brief lesson about the Yale University seal could be helpful here. On the seal, words appear in both Hebrew and Latin. First, Yale's seal centers an open book with the Hebrew words *urim* and *thummim*. The book rests in a blue shield. Below the shield, a scroll with the Latin words, Lux et Veritas, waves. The two sets of words are equivalent in meaning, and both translate into English as light and truth. A 1578 Genevan Bible, available at Yale when the crest was created, explained, "Urim signifieth light and Thummim perfection: declaring that the stones of the brestplate were most cleare, and of perfect beautie: by Urim also is ment knowledge & Thummim holiness, shewing what virtues are required in the Priests."[101] Perhaps these symbols were included in the Yale crest to inspire students to reach for the highest learning and ideals as they studied, or at least that's how my father seemed to teach the motto to me. Light and truth were about seeking not only knowledge but acting intelligently. Not only having light but using its power with respect.

In 1726 all Yale students studied divinity using Johannes Wollebius's *The Abridgement of Christian Divinitie*, which explained, "Urim and Thummim…

did signify Christ the Word and Interpreter of the Father, our light and perfection."[102] Let's try to apply this explanation to the goal James has challenged us with: be perfect. And how do we become perfect? James tells us to seek light and truth, or to seek Christ. Christ will show us the way (provide light to the path) and help us understand the will of our Father (perfect us) through good gifts from above.

I can hear you saying, "It's not that easy! You can't just seek God and become perfect." In fact, there is only one example of perfection available to us, which is the life of Christ as written in the New Testament, and I'm not that good! James understood this dilemma, and he knows that he is not perfect either. He didn't even accept his own brother's mission and divine calling until after His death. Despite all the learning and all the conversations with his brother while growing up, all James's knowledge from the Hebrew Scriptures about the Messiah coming to save His people discussed at home, James just didn't jump-in right away. But he did finally understand something, and that is what he is sharing in his epistle.

Throughout the Old Testament, James knew that the prophets continually reviewed and repeated the history of the children of Israel. The stories of the Bible present us with a variety of flawed human decisions. And yet, almost every story encourages us that God does not forget His people. We learn the paths of God by learning the stories of His children, sometimes by positive examples and sometimes by negative example. Thus "not by means of abstract formulae does [the Bible] bring God and duty to the soul of man, but by means of lives of human beings who feel and fail, who stumble and sin as we do; yet who, in their darkest groping, remain conscious of the one true way—and rise again."[103] We will not be perfect in every action. We are human. But "if you ever wonder how in the world God could use you to change the world, look at these people"[104] in the Old and New Testaments. Even the prophets have moments of doubt, now and again. But they use their weak moments to increase their faith (James 1:2). If we allow our faith to develop, trials will work a perfect faith. As we seek the ideals presented in the Law and covenants of God, we will gain a unique perspective. God will use our flaws to help us develop strengths; He will use our weaknesses to perfect others. What we need is the ability to discern God's will first for ourselves and then to discern how we might assist Him in His work.

I understand a little bit about James not really accepting the truths Jesus offered him while they were growing-up. As my husband and I were preparing for the arrival of our first child, we moved close to my parents. I had been gone from the area since I graduated from high school. I had changed, gone to college, learned a few things, gotten married. Well, you get the picture. What made this return difficult was how I felt people who knew me before were treating me. In their minds I was still a teenager, and they remembered every ugly learning experience I had. One woman chose to act differently. She invited me to museums and asked me to teach her about the art. She arranged for me to meet socially new people to the area. She connected me with a book group. I'm sure she had doubts about my teenage choices, but you never would have known it from the way she treated me. With God on her side, this sweet woman helped me be accepted by others for my strengths and not my past. In retrospect, I was letting my insecurities appear as truth and got offended by what I thought others were thinking about me. This woman thought better of me and helped me correct my harmful personal judgments. In doing so she helped me increase my faith in others and in the power of God to answer my prayers for new friends. When I think about my past and about this woman particularly, I remember her kindness and want to retrieve any and all negative things I ever said or thought about her. And so I strive to give people fresh starts, keeping in mind the motto, *it's never too late to start your life over*.

Back in James 1:17-18, where James talks of light and truth together, I think James is using these verses to also teach us of our divine worth. First, we learn that God allowed each of us to have birth through the Word of Truth. This refers to the spiritual birth individuals can enjoy when they accept Christ (God's Word) into their lives. Secondly, James says that we can be like first fruits. Paul refers to "Christ the first fruits," or the first to be resurrected, and he assures us that every man in his own order will enjoy that blessing at Christ's coming.[105] We will become resurrected beings. Using the translation of James from the Amplified Bible, James suggests in verse 18 that a type of consecration is necessary for us before we can realize the blessing of being part of the first fruits. Consecration is synonymous with dedication and purity. Thus, this verse can be understood to say that God has provided a way for us to be spiritually born and become consecrated toward achieving eternal life—a way to find meaning in the atonement of the Savior and dedicate ourselves to becoming perfect.

In these verses, then, James teaches the gospel of Jesus Christ. He explains, like Yale's eighteenth-century guide to Christians, that we must let Christ teach us knowledge and give us perfection. In other words, James encourages us to accept the blessings of the gospel and the work that Christ came to do, namely to atone for our sins. James recognizes that Christ's atonement is designed to free us from error, give us power to resist temptation, and help us be ready to receive the gift of forgiveness. "The rest of the letter then proceeds to describe the dimensions of this Christian existence, which requires a continual hearing of and obedience to God's word."[106]

In accepting Christ as our Savior, we accept the light and truth of the gospel. John explained the outcome of this pursuit in his first general epistle: "Beloved, now are we the sons of God,…but we know that, when he shall appear, we shall be like him; for we shall see him as he is…."[107] In other words, we will see Jesus Christ as He is: the light and perfection of His Father.

Sorting and Bundling: Integrative Questions for Reflection

What do you think are the key events in the life of Jesus?

Write about what you think Jesus Christ accomplished during his life (what was his mission)?

What do you believe about Jesus the Christ?

Describe your relationship with God.

What does it mean to be spiritually born?

Define the words: *consecration*, *dedication*, and *purity*. Would you use these words to describe yourself? Why or why not?

What occurred during the atonement of Jesus Christ?

How do the events/blessings of the atonement affect you?

Write an action step of something you can start today to gain more light and truth about the meaning of the atonement in your own life.

_____

_____

_____

Finding Current Applications of James's Challenge

In the introductory comments to a recent collection of stories about greatness, Stephen Covey suggests that greatness comes from three choices:

1. Choice to act…and not be acted upon

2. Choice of purpose…to what end will our daily choices lead?

3. Choice of principles…will we live in accordance with proven principles?[108]

These guidelines provide an interesting measuring stick with which we can compare the greatness of what James presents about Christ's ultimate sacrifice: His atonement.

First, no one forces me to accept the atonement. If I believe in its power then I can choose to accept it as real and life-changing. If I do not accept its power then I still continue to choose my actions and I am still accountable for those choices.

Second, the atonement has a purpose. Through it, Christ met the requirements and demands of justice, and He offers each of us mercy.

Third, the atonement presents true principles. When Christ went to the garden of Gethsemane to begin the atonement, he brought three of His apostles. He asked them to remain as He went a little farther alone, and He cautioned Peter, James, and John to "pray, that ye enter not into temptation." When Christ returns to them, He awakens them and repeats His advice and then adds, "The spirit indeed is willing, but the flesh is weak."[109] With this expression, we can hear both admission from Christ of His intentions and His counsel to His apostles. He admits that His spirit is willing to make this ultimate sacrifice but that His earthly body is weak. His counsel instructs His apostles to train their minds, pray: be spiritual and seek the light of God; and to train their bodies, avoiding temptation: physically act as they had seen Christ act. In accepting the atonement, we agree to take the same challenge given the apostles, to train our minds and bodies, to seek light and truth. When James teaches about the atonement, he teaches about faith, repentance, and the influence of the Spirit. Faith in the power of atonement takes time to develop. To extend my faith in the atonement, I need to seek the wisdom that God offers. To act on this faith, I need to imitate the unconditional love God has for all His children in my daily actions and judgments. When I fail, I can renew my commitments and try again. Christ can be my interpreter of God and of His will for me.

The question now falls to each of us, knowing the blessings of the atonement, am I willing to commit to living by a higher standard and seek perfection?

It is interesting that the symbols of covenant and commitments with God are often so simple—to be so easily seen but not understood with a deeper meaning unless we really seek to understand and/or see with spiritual eyes. So light is light, which is something that allows us to see—or it is understanding the wisdom that God has to share about seeking eternal life. Truth is truth, some lofty concept that we talk about but will never grasp—or it is about trying to act like Christ and to have Christlike love for all mankind. Perfection is perfection, an ideal that is too far away for me to realistically aim for—or it is a commitment to seek light and truth, accepting the power of the atonement in our lives and commit to change.

In Hosea, the prophet shares the story of his wayward wife and how he tried to coax her to return. Hosea uses the objects bread-water, wool-flax, and oil-drink. All are given to the wife, hoping that she would recognize her errors and return to her loving husband. The relationship between the two is clear, but it also represents Israel and God. The bread and water are vital to sustaining life, but they are also symbols of sacrifice, specifically the sacrament of the Lord's Last Supper, and our covenant with God that we accept Christ in our lives. The wool and flax are needed to provide clothing, but they are also about covering our nakedness, reminding us of the covenant God made with Adam when he was expelled from the garden of Eden.[110] The oil and drink are outward signs of wealth, but they are also necessary for healing and soothing injures and for anointing the dead, reminding us that we all need an advocate who has the ability to comfort us in times of trouble, or someone who can answer the demands of justice when we fall short.

James was familiar with the Scriptures. He spent time reading and studying. He knew that symbols could help us be enlightened. Although he does not use the same symbols as Hosea, he certainly displays a similar use of simple-to-deeper meanings that becomes apparent if we study his epistle.

I have believed in Jesus Christ and a loving heavenly Father as long as I can remember. I have never really questioned whether they existed or not; I felt like they did. The big question for me was whether I was worthy of their attention and effort at any given time. I think my deepest worry has occurred when my life was not going the way I thought it would go and when I assumed that I was due different blessings than I was receiving. Thus my doubts were more about whether I was good enough to receive what I believed were prized blessings. But in seeking for light and truth, I have learned that my conclusions were faulty; it was never about me being good enough or me receiving greater blessings, because God is not comparing me to anyone else but me. He wants me to know that when I receive a new teaching, I study it out in my mind, find its application through my heart, and make the visceral commitment to act. The wisdom of seeking perfection requires me to abandon the idea that I am to compare myself against some unattainable ideal, and I must instead measure my steps toward perfection against the teachings and knowledge I have received up to this point in my life. I need to train my mind to this way of thinking, for this is intelligence.

Moses Maimonides, a medieval Jewish scholar, stated "that it must be man's aim, after having acquired the knowledge of God, to deliver himself up to Him, and to have his heart constantly filled with longing after Him."[111] He goes on to provide steps for educating and training your mind to attain a perfect knowledge of God:

1. When you embark on a task, turn your thoughts away from everything else and be present.

2. Focus on what you are doing. Give your present task both your heart and mind, especially a religious service.

3. When alone, meditate on how you should approach God and how best to minister before Him.

4. When you gain true knowledge, be grateful and thank God.

5. When you stumble over obstacles, recognize that they are of your own construction and that somehow you chose to separate yourself from God.[112]

I am fascinated that his advice seems so modern and perhaps a little New Age. And yet Maimonides is closer (historically) to the life of the Savior than I am, and so I wonder sometimes what practices we may have lost through time. For example, my grandmother wrote letters to me and cut out newspaper articles when she wanted to give me advice; today, grandmothers send e-mails and attach files. Communication is still occurring; the method is just different. And so, again, I wonder in the passage of time how things have changed and how their purposes remain the same.

Light and truth can remain lofty concepts that are worthy of study by philosophers only, or we can enter the conversation. Seeking light and truth can forever be beyond our reach, or we can begin to train our minds and bodies to be more aware of their influence. Light and truth can be just a university motto, or it can become a personal motto and statement of intention. To seek light and truth is to seek after the ways of God, to understand His purposes, and to qualify to receive the gifts He wants to give. To have light and truth is to accept the Gospel of Jesus Christ and His atoning sacrifice. The Gospel of Jesus Christ may be preached to the masses, but it is internalized individually; its ordinances may be universal, but we covenant with God individually. The atonement is available to all, but it is accepted personally. To qualify for the gift of becoming perfect and whole, we must seek for light and truth personally, and when we receive an increase of knowledge, we are responsible to act on what we have learned.

Sorting and Bundling: Integrative Questions for Reflection

What are some of the teachings of Christ that resonate with you?

Do you live any of the above listed teachings perfectly?

How might you better live up to the teachings you listed above?

Review Moses Maimonides's steps to gain more perfect knowledge of God. How could you use these ideas in your daily life?

Make a list of the gifts that you recognize God has given to you and to others that are close to you.

Have you ever thought about seeking and asking God for any of the gifts you listed above?

What would you need to do in your life to become eligible to receive specific gifts from God?

Lyn Bair

LIVING THE WHOLE (ROYAL) LAW (OF LIBERTY)

> There remain some famous and still-baffling conundrums, which have obsessed and frustrated generations of would-be solvers. And each problem that is solved potentially raises hundreds more…[113]

Throughout his epistle, James demonstrates his knowledge of the Torah, recalling the language of the prophets. He knows the history of the Jewish people. He understands the Law of Moses and its penalties. He also has accepted an oral tradition taught by his brother, Jesus, and so he perceives a broader application of the law than may be available in Old Testament books of Scripture. All these elements are blended into the epistle such that without some searching, the ideas almost appear fresh and singular.

James's ideas, however, are really not new; they are simply presented in a way that we may not have become familiar. For example, in the book of Genesis, we read a story of Jacob where he is told to "be clean, and change your garments." [114] From this statement, one might assume that they should wash and put on clean clothes. But Jacob does not perceive a literal message but something greater and chooses to take his family to Beth-el, the site of an earlier spiritual experience and vision for him. What is it about the message that causes Jacob to act the way he does?

Early in the Epistle of James, the author gives his readers a goal: "Be perfect and entire." If we take this as literal instruction, we reason its impossibility and mock the charge given. But if we see this as spiritual instruction, we, like the Prophet Jacob, will try to remember lessons from our past and seek to follow through with the commitments we made at an earlier time.

In the story of Jacob, he returns to Beth-el, and the Abrahamic covenant is renewed with him. Blessings of land, seed, and influence are promised to Jacob, just as they had been promised to Isaac and Abraham. Jacob recalls his earlier spiritual experience and recognizes that these promises were made to him years before in his first visit to this place.[115] At that time he made a personal commitment to act so the Lord would be with him.

James follows the pattern given in the book of Genesis, hoping that we will see past the mere words of his instruction and recall previous commitments that we have made spiritually. Instead of the Lord charging His prophet with instructions and blessings, James prophetically charges the followers of the Lord with instructions and blessings. From the structure of his epistle, it seems that James hopes that we will understand that a "tried" faith in the Lord Jesus Christ is our gateway to achieving perfection.

Once we renew our resolve to serve Jesus, then the next logical steps involve us seeking perfection. In this quest, however, our author does not leave us without direction. He suggests that we develop two qualities that he believes will be helpful in accomplishing his stated goal; first, we must seek wisdom (light). And second, we must learn to love others without judgment (perfection).

James speaks to his audience, the dispersed tribes of Israel, as if their religious training has been similar to his own. He assumes therefore that they will understand his meaning and can put both the stories he cites and the language he uses into proper context. We know that the "word of God is living and active"[116] and that it has power to speak to us today, even though "we hear not as first-century Christians...but as men and women alive here and now."[117] We will, therefore, need to take time to study, ask some questions, look for translations and interpretations that may help, and seek to understand the words, context, and principles that are taught by James if we hope to feel the Spirit behind the words of his text.

I love to read historical fiction. There is something about the story being partly true that intrigues me. I especially like to read great place-descriptions and really enjoy sitting in art history lectures when the professor provides location information. Like, when you are standing in the Grand Gallery of the Louvre, look this way or that to find this painting. I suppose that part of this fascination is about me connecting to where something important may have occurred. For example, while standing in the Roman Forum with my family, we read a scene from Shakespeare's *Julius Ceasar*, and I tried to get them to see the event happening right where we were standing. Moments like these can be very moving for me, and they help my imagination see possible scenarios.

Sometimes we visit monuments and can feel a reverent presence. I recall traveling to Assisi with a group of high school students, we were headed to the main church when one of my students stopped me, and said, "I don't feel like I'm good enough to be here, maybe I should just wait on this bench for you to return." Wow, while I was glad he felt something in that environment, I assured him, based on what I know about Saint Francis of Assisi, that his presence would not harm the church or anyone around him, but instead the church might actually return something to him based on what he was looking for. He came with me, never being very far from my side. When we returned home, this young man was different. No more interruptions in class, he stopped wearing his baseball cap all the time, and he was generally kinder to his peers. There was power in Assisi for that young man, a power that helped him begin making changes in his life. Personally, I think he experienced a spiritual connection with the kindness and simplicity of St. Francis's message, and his connection had a lot to do with being in the same place where St. Francis had experienced so much of his own spiritual growth.

Sorting and Bundling:
Integrative Questions for Reflection

What do you think the Lord's instruction to Jacob means ("be clean, and change your garments")?

Make a list of a few of the spiritual lessons you have learned.

Do you remember when and where you first learned the lessons of the above list? Write about your memories.

Do you remember the way you felt when these spiritual truths first made sense to you? Write about at least one specific experience.

Have you ever visited or returned to a specific place to regain the power of what happened spiritually there?

_____

_____

_____

The Law of Moses

Based on what we know of James's background, we believe he was taught the Law of Moses. He knows the rules and statutes detailed in Exodus and Leviticus. He understands the penalties assigned if the law is not obeyed. The word *law*, when related to Scripture, refers to "the body of commandments which express the will of God with regard to the conduct of His... people."[118] When James speaks of the Law of Moses, he uses simply the word *law*. For James, this represents all the written laws given to Moses for the children of Israel; these laws had specific requirements, rituals, and ceremonies.

In Exodus chapters 15-19, we learn about the conversion of the children of Israel. Through Moses, God offers a covenant to the children of Israel. They all say yes—three different times they say yes—but before the covenant is even written by the hand of God, they begin to worship other gods and dishonor themselves, thereby breaking the covenant. Moses sees this worship and physically breaks the tables that have been issued for him to provide further instruction. When Moses tries to atone for the sins of the people, God instructs him that each man must pay for his own sins.

And then God does something that is different; instead of continuing to lead His people directly, He sends an angel to accompany the people on their journey. This is a layer of separation, to only be in the presence of angels and no longer in the company of God. Remember that God is now referring to the children of Israel as Moses's people; that certainly is a level of separation. Is it possible that the second set of tablets God issues also represents a layer of separation? Somehow the law of God is changed on the second set of tables and is now referred to as the Law of Moses. Hence, the children of Israel are led by an angel, called the people of Moses, and are under covenant to keep the Law of Moses.

Combine this background with teachings from the New Testament. Presumably all the authors were called of God and either had direct experience with Jesus or were taught through visions by Jesus. Paul may explain the best the Christian interpretation of the law in his epistle to the Galatians. He says that the Law of Moses was "added because of transgressions, till the seed [Christ] should come to whom the promise was made."[119] The law was added because of transgression? Is Paul saying because the children of Israel transgressed the covenant they made with God the Law of Moses was added? Added to what? Furthermore, it sounds like the Law of Moses was only temporary, since Paul says, "Till…[Christ] should come." At the very end of his explanation, Paul suggests that Christ would come to those to whom the promise was made. Who is this? Then Paul goes on to say, "But before faith came, we were kept under the law.… Wherefore the law was our schoolmaster to bring us unto Christ.…"[120] The chiasm of this statement confirms that the law was only meant to be temporary and that it was a training tool that would prepare us to have faith in Christ. Thus, from these passages we learn that the "faith-principle is older and more fundamental than the Mosaic law."[121] What if the original covenant was based on faith in Christ and contained a promise that Christ would come to those who believed, thereby fulfilling part of the covenant?

I can't determine from Scripture what the terms of the covenant, made to the house of Israel, were originally. But I suspect that it may have been a renewal of the covenant made with Noah[122], Abraham,[123] Isaac,[124] and renewed again with Jacob,[125] who became Israel. It seems logical that God would renew the covenant yet again with a freed people of Israel. Could it be that the first set of tablets contained the words and promises of this renewed covenant? Has this covenant that God keeps renewing always been based on faith in Jesus the Christ, the Messiah?

If the second set of tablets were edited by God, as many biblical scholars suggest, to contain a more fundamental part of His covenant, something more rudimentary with a level of separation from the original, a schoolmaster meant to prepare us for more, then it is the second set of tablets that contained what the Israelites used to guide their religious services and personal actions, the second set of tablets becomes what we know as the Law of Moses.

Because James's religious education was supplemented by conversations and teaching of Jesus, he understood the historical and spiritual nature of the Law of Moses, and he accepted Jesus as the fulfillment of both the law and of the faith-based covenant that God continues to renew with His people. It is from this context that James speaks of the law.

Sorting and Bundling: Integrative Questions for Reflection

What do you think was written on the first set of tablets that Moses brought down from God to the people of Israel?

Have you ever been resolute with a decision, only to have everything fall apart later? How do you pick yourself up after you backslide to regain your original level of resolve?

What levels of separation keep you away from God?

What might you do to reduce the levels of separation between you and God?

What are the implications of accepting that the first set of tablets contained the words of the covenant made with Adam, Noah, Abraham, and other prophets?

How can you be more connected to the faith-based covenant? Write an action plan for one thing you can do today that would demonstrate your understanding about faith and about covenants.

_____

_____

_____

The Law of Liberty

James refers to the law and its penalties in the second chapter of his epistle, explaining, "Yet offend in one point, he is guilty of all"[126] or that when you violate even one small part of the law, in effect you have violated the whole law and are accountable to all its penalties.

But then James writes, "So speak ye, and so do."[127] At first, I wonder if he is reminding us of the lack of commitment given by the children of Israel at the base of Mount Sinai by people who agreed to the covenant by word but who acted differently than they spoke. But then I think, since this time he lacks detailing the punishment, I wonder if James is offering a counter example to the Law of Moses. Instead of being held to the strictness of the law, we are accountable to the law of liberty. On one hand, the children of Israel agreed to a covenant and were therefore accountable to the statutes and penalties of the law. But for those on the other hand, those that are held accountable to the law of liberty, we assume that they also would have to agree to some covenant. These people would have accepted the law of liberty as their standard, instead of the Law of Moses. So what is their covenant?

Although James does not state it specifically, he does state that the law of liberty offers mercy that "rejoiceth against judgment," which he contrasts to the law that is "judgment without mercy."[128] This is where James begins to show his readers the difference between Moses's Law and Christ's law of liberty. The two laws clearly have differences, but we need to continue through the epistle to better understand what James is offering.

As if James is writing an expository essay, his epistle proceeds with a second piece of support; this time it's a comparison between faith and works. Here he connects the law to works or works of the law while connecting faith with the law of liberty. His conclusion now is that faith without works is dead. And I believe that James would accept the converse as well that works without faith is dead. James knows that his readers know that the Law of Moses requires specific rituals and ceremonies (works), and yet he is trying to expand their view to understand that unless they have faith in the law of liberty, their rituals alone will not save them. At the same time, it seems clear that to only show faith is also not sufficient if our actions do not reflect what we say ("so speak ye, and so do").[129]

Then James gives his third and final piece of support of scriptural examples of Abraham and Rahab. The first has faith. "He believed in the Lord,"[130] and he chose to be obedient to God's commands despite their difficulty and his own pain. Rahab, on the other hand, lacks religious training but made a choice based on a belief that "he is God in heaven above and earth beneath,"[131] and she therefore offers protection and aid to the children of Israel in overtaking Jericho. From these two examples, I learn that regardless of whether you are under covenant or not, when you can choose well, your actions will demonstrate your faith; Jews and Gentiles both have access to the law of liberty and can both be faithful to God through their actions.

A quick summary of the points that James makes in his second chapter can be seen to the following columns:

Law	*Law of Liberty*
Judgment with mercy	Mercy against judgment
Works (do all that is required)	Faith to obey and act well
Access to covenant promises	Access to covenant promises

Is there an advantage to following one law over the other? I believe James has stacked up evidence to suggest that while both are important, the law of liberty is broader in its tolerance and love.

Earlier in his epistle, James proclaimed that those who look into the perfect law of liberty must be hearers of the word and doers of the work. Sometimes God asks us to do small things. Once as a young mother, I felt impressed to check on my napping toddler. I didn't think much of the impression at first, but I did take a

From Straw to Pillar

quick peek; all was fine. A little later that same day, I felt like I needed to check on an elderly neighbor. But this time I resisted, not wanting to wake the baby, and I pushed the idea out of my mind. Not long after thinking this, the phone rang, and, yes, it was my neighbor; she needed my help. She hadn't wanted to bother me, but she was in a bind and really needed some help and wondered if I could come over right away. God really only needed me to do a very small thing. I suppose my actions were a little like the children of Israel who were asked to simply look upon the brazen serpent lifted on a staff,[132] if they hoped to be saved. And like many of the Israelites, I had to be bitten a couple of times before I lifted my eyes and looked; I heard the word but needed encouragement to do the work.

There are many small things that we can do. They don't take much effort, but how resistant are we to spiritual promptings? Keeping the Sabbath is a small thing, but do we do it? Taking time during our day to be still and listen, and to pray and meditate, is a small thing, but do we do it? To smile at someone else or say hello are small things, but do we make the effort? How much time and/or effort would it actually take for us to choose to do some very simple things that would show our empathy for our fellowmen and love for our neighbors?

My neighbor was fine that day, but I learned a valuable lesson that sometimes small things can make a big difference. Since I know I should love my neighbor (I've heard the word), can I also do the work that is necessary to demonstrate what I know (be a doer of the work)?

Sorting and Bundling:
Integrative Questions for Reflection

What do you think the Law of Liberty is? How does the Law of Liberty differ from the Law of Moses?

Name some "small" things God has asked you to do?

What methods has God employed to help you hear His requests?

Could you improve your ability to hear God's requests? How might you do that?

What could you do to more quickly respond to God's spiritual promptings?

_____

_____

_____

The Royal Law

"If ye fulfill the royal law according to the scripture, Thou shalt love thy neighbor as thyself."[133] At first it may seem easy to fulfill the royal law, all that is needed is to love your neighbor. Yet on further investigation, the Royal Law is a bit more complex. From the structure of his argument, I think James has found another way to repeat his original goal: be perfect by seeking for light and truth, but this time he says, keep the royal law by abiding the requirements of law and showing faith with action. In the structure of his epistle, James connects the following ideas:

1. Seeking perfection = keeping the royal law
2. Wisdom, light, the will of God, and action = law
3. Truth, love without judgment, discernment, faith = law of liberty

Thus, James presents the ideal situation first and then provides examples to convince us that living the royal law is a combination of knowing the law and choosing the law of liberty.

James's Jewish readers would have been familiar with the charge to "love thy neighbor as thyself."[134] They also would have rehearsed the many things the Lord required them to do: "Fear the Lord...walk in all his ways...love...serve...with all thy heart and...soul, to keep the commandments...and his statutes.... Love therefore the stranger: for ye were strangers in the land of Egypt."[135] James's message isn't that different from what his readers had been taught; the twist comes in that he calls it the royal law, and James wants them to recognize and have faith in Jesus Christ. James needs his readers to know that the Messiah was Jesus and that he had come to them to fulfill the covenant that God made with their fathers. James wants his readers to accept that they had been offered the covenant and promise spoken of in Scripture and that Abraham's seed, Christ, had fulfilled the promise.

The stumbling block for James's readers of the first century (and for Paul's Galatian converts) was twofold: accept Christ as the rock of their salvation and know that the Law of Moses had been fulfilled by Jesus, His actions, and His sacrifice, and was therefore no longer binding. These first-century followers had to let go of a training tool and develop personal faith. We, on the other hand, think, *No problem, I accept Christ, and I have faith in salvation, but no way can I do all these things necessary to attain perfection.* Our stumbling block is a modern interpretation of a word.

James teaches that to keep the royal law, we are to love our neighbors as ourselves. This imperative is shortly followed by additional advice where James tells us to hear the Word of God and to do the work of God. We should hear, love our neighbors and be sure to help those in need.[136] We should accept, there is one lawgiver and stop judging others based on external measures.[137] We should internalize the teachings of Christ by thinking of others as we pray and bear testimony of the truth of the gospel.[138] By combining various ideas in his epistle, James tenderly teaches us how to live the whole royal law. As we study his comparisons and contrasts, we need to recognize that to keep the royal law requires us to both do all of God's requirements and also to accept and have faith in Jesus as our Redeemer. Here are some of the combinations James provides for us to learn about the royal law:

> Wisdom and Non-judgment (1:5; 2:1-6)
>
> Hear and Do (1:19-24)
>
> Choose and Be Accountable (1:6-10; 2:9-11)
>
> Mercy and Judgment (2:13)
>
> Speak and So Do (2:12)
>
> Faith and Works (2:14-26)
>
> Control and Wisdom (3:1-17)
>
> Friendship and Humility (2:23, 4:10)
>
> Doers not Judges (4:11-15)
>
> Patience and Gratitude (5:7-11)
>
> Prayer and Belief (5:13-20)
>
> Love and Perfection (1:1-5:20)

Just like the comparisons James presents, the royal law brings the law and the law of liberty together. It combines ideas, making each idea richer. The royal law gives us hope. In the "Divine Comedy," James tests the main character about hope; during the examination Dante responds that his ideas have been instilled from James's epistle, and he states:

> Hope is the certain expectation
> of future glory; it is the result
> of God's grace and of merit we have earned.
> …The new and ancient Scriptures set
> the mark for souls whom God befriends; for me,
> that mark means what is promised us by hope.[139]

Dante's explanation of hope, that he claimed was taught in the Epistle of James, is a very good summary of the whole royal law. This Renaissance author understood that both ancient and new Scripture promised us future glory as the result of what we had earned by our actions combined with the grace of God. I submit that Dante was expressing his belief in the promises of the royal law as taught in ancient and new Scripture, that it gives us hope unto salvation.

In ancient Scripture, we know that Abraham made a covenant with God where he was given great blessings, a future glory if you will, and we know that to receive these blessings, Abraham was expected to act with faith and be obedient to God's request to sacrifice his own heir and son. But before Abraham, we know that Noah made a covenant with God that also promised future glory. Noah "did according unto all that the Lord commanded him,"[140] and his actions showed the faith he had in God and in God's promises. I wonder whether Adam and all of his descendants down to Noah were offered the same covenant and blessing: hope in a future glory, opportunity to be called the sons of God, and the promise that Christ would come to those who believed in His role as the Savior and Redeemer.

If this covenant was made anciently with prophets, and would be fulfilled when Christ came to those who believed, then the covenant is still in force today. Yes, we believe that Christ came to the earth and fulfilled his mission of teaching and completed the atonement. For those alive at the meridian of time, Christ came and fulfilled the promise made in the covenant. Modern-day Christians continue to hope for salvation through Christ and they continue to look forward to His second coming, when they will be able to experience the fulfillment of the blessings promised in the covenant for themselves. Thus, the original covenant made with Adam has been renewed via many prophets through time. This covenant is still available to us today by living the gospel of Jesus Christ and seeking the blessings of His atonement. When we live the Whole Royal Law of Liberty we are participating in the spirit of this covenant.

What must we do to keep this whole royal law of liberty? First, I believe that we must be like Abraham and actively seek the blessings of the ancient ones. Although these blessings were available at one point, when God tried to renew the covenant with the children of Israel, they demonstrated that they were not ready, and so God provided the law to teach them about obedience. Scripture teaches us that the Law of Moses was meant to be temporary and that Christ was to fulfill the law. Remember that Moses tried to be punished for the sins of his people, but God told him that each person was responsible for their own errors. Christ, however, suffered for the sins of all people, thus, part of His mission was to make up the difference between our own repentance and the demands of justice. We are each responsible to make necessary changes in our lives, to repent, if you will, from errors in judgment and action. James teaches us that obeying the royal law is about having faith in Christ's atonement and his role as Redeemer, and loving our neighbors. Thus the royal law brings our faith and works together producing perfection, righteousness, and friendship with God.

When I suggest that we must search like Abraham, I'm suggesting that we must look for light and truth, and for wisdom and understanding. Abraham knew that to be perfect in God's eyes, he needed to be kind to strangers and show his faith through his obedience to God's commands. Abraham knew, accepted, and lived the royal law of liberty.

The law was about being individually responsible for our errors and correcting those errors through ritual and sacrifice. The law of liberty was about making good choices based on the light and knowledge we had acquired. The royal law gave us an imperative to love our neighbors as ourselves. When we live the whole royal law of liberty, we embrace accountability, agency, and love as our guiding principles.

Sorting and Bundling: Integrative Questions for Reflection

Can you identify some of your own stumbling blocks, issues interfering with you living closer to God?

How do you show your neighbors that you love and care for them?

Review the list above of the tenets of the Royal Law. Reread the scriptural references provided. Of the twelve items, which do you already understand? Which do you need to study?

If the key blessing of living the Royal Law is future glory, what will this blessing include?

What are some of your guiding principles?

What can you do to bring your guiding principles closer to the will of God?

How would aligning your guiding principles with the will of God demonstrate living the whole royal law?

Lyn Bair

LESSONS BY EXAMPLE: ABRAHAM, RAHAB, JOB, AND ELIJAH

> The learner must be lead always from familiar objects toward the unfamiliar, guided along, as it were, a chain of flowers into the mysteries of life.
>
> —Charles Wilson Peale

Storytellers have great appeal to me. They spin yarns (where did that expression come from?), entertain, and teach. Not every story I hear makes an impact, so I wonder what is it that makes some of the stories different, easy to remember, and charming? Is it the characters, the plot or the setting, or maybe it's just the moral of the story? Sometimes it takes several times hearing a story before I begin to get any insight or meaning in it. Sometimes I recognize a character type, for example the hero, and can then compare the elements of this story to others I know.

There are some historical people that we know enough about from stories that we use their names as references to bigger ideas or concepts. Some names allow us to think of virtues, concepts, and/or specific places or events. They can even give us reason to picture scenes or perhaps travel to other countries. The power of a strong character widens our minds and invites different memories and images.

James relies on the power of our minds to recall information, to compare and contrast, and to fill in the gaps to complete stories when he briefly mentions four biblical names in his epistle: Abraham, Rahab, Job, and Elijah. This is a different combination than others I have read. What stories does James believe we have access to? Why has he chosen this combination of names? First let's do some individual investigations, and then we'll start comparing and contrasting.

Who Are These People?

Abraham is well-known and seen as the patriarch of Jews and Muslims and Christians. *National Geographic* featured Abraham with a forty-page cover story in 2001 stating, "The important thing, we are told, is to assess the meaning and legacy of the ideas Abraham came to embody."[141] Abraham's story occurs in Genesis, starting in chapter eleven. Over 100 references to Abram/Abraham occur in sixteen Old Testament books and eleven New Testament books (that's 41 percent of biblical books); these stories "describe his hospitality and peaceableness and, most importantly, his faith and obedience to God."[142] James would have known the importance of this prophet; he would have known details of his life and accomplishments, and he certainly would have accepted him as the father of the covenant.

Rahab is less well-known than Abraham, but that does not diminish her story. Rahab was an innkeeper living in Jericho. Before Joshua conquered the city, he sent spies to gather information. Rahab, a woman with a questionable career, assists these spies and promises to help them later during their impending conquest.

James would have known the genealogy of his own family, which includes lineages that are detailed by Matthew. Matthew starts with a genealogy because he wants us to know who Christ is and where he came from, specifically: Abraham, Isaac, Jacob, Jesse, King David, King Solomon, and Joseph, the father of James and husband of Mary, the mother of Jesus. James would have connected himself directly to Abraham as an ancestor and as a religious father, and he would have known that Rahab occupied the place of a maternal ancestor (one of five women mentioned by Matthew). James uses these first two people, both from the royal lineage of Christ, as spiritual examples of faith. Perhaps James is inviting us to consider both our literal genealogy and our spiritual genealogy. Do you know where you come from? Which genealogy is more important to you? To whom do we owe allegiance? Is there strength in being connected to a great name?

Job was a successful man with family, property, and community prestige, and he knew he owed his success to God. He is the object of a biblical experiment, testing whether he would still be a faithful follower of God if he were to lose all his measures of earthly success. In terms of writing, the text of the book of Job is considered to be part of the Jewish wisdom literature, and it also compares with Egyptian and Babylonian wisdom writings.

> The Wise in Israel sought to understand God and his ways by studying the great uniformities

of human experience.... Proverbs is a typical example of their understanding of life. Job is a flaming protest, less against the basic concept of Proverbs that a God-fearing life brings prosperity, godlessness suffering and destruction, than against the idea that thereby the ways of God are fully grasped. Job is not a type; he is an exception that makes folly of the assumption that through normal experience the depths of God's wisdom and working can be fully grasped.[143]

Job's text teaches us that God is more powerful than we can imagine, and Job's story teaches us the merits of having personal integrity and patience as we experience trials and gain new awareness in our lives.

Elijah, the fourth example James uses, is an important prophet for the Jewish people. Six episodes from the life of Elijah are presented biblically: his prediction of drought, the contest on Mt. Carmel, the flight to Horeb, the Naboth incident, the oracle about Ahaziah, and his translation into heaven. A common theme in all of these episodes is a conflict with King Ahab and his wife, Jezebel, and their worship of Baal. Elijah's ministry is one where the people of Israel are reminded "both in worshipping Yahweh alone as well as in proclaiming Mosaic standards of righteousness in the community."[144]

James uses the examples of Job and Elijah, men who knew and followed the will of God despite criticism and trials, when telling his readers about how to be part of a community. I think James is challenging us to be the same people with our community members as we try to be with God, instead of being one person at church and someone else in business.

So how does James use his four examples, and what specific lesson is he teaching? Is he teaching about heritage and authenticity? Perhaps he is citing examples that are teaching us what to do and how to be? He provides the name of a specific person and assumes we know their whole story; he teaches us big concepts using individual examples, and he assumes we know his meaning.

This reminds me of general teaching. Teachers give large groups of students the same information; they may provide several specific examples and demonstrate skills until most questions have been satisfied. Teachers share their insights, experiences, and "aha" moments. But each student must learn the skills, knowledge, and counsel imparted individually. Once the lessons are internalized, then the student can access the information learned and use it to his/her advantage. Since not all students have exactly the same background knowledge, some see connections to other pieces of information, and others do not. Thus, we teach broad concepts using specific examples. The number of examples used will depend on the grouping of students. James must have thought most of us would have grasped his meaning by the time he shared his fourth example and would have sufficient background knowledge so that his four examples would create the right mindset. This collection of names teaches us a variety of things that are detailed in the next sections.

First Things First

I see some important firsts in this group of four names. Abraham is a key name in both God's covenant with man and in the ancestral line of people all over the world. He represents an entry point of faith heritage and family genealogy. Rahab is one of the first gentiles to accept the God of Israel and plays a key role helping the children of Israel enter into the promised land. Her actions allow for the first recovery of the Abrahamic inheritance (land). Job is a first in wisdom literature, whether a real man or merely a moral story figure, as he goes through the course of his story, his understanding of God's greatness grows. In the end, Job accepts God's will, knows the truth of the Redeemer, seeks remission of his flaws, and desires to show faithfulness in a powerful yet merciful God. Elijah prepares his people for the first coming of the Messiah. His story encourages the children of Israel to return to the original invitation and covenant God offered them. He demonstrates that when our first priority is to know and do God's will, we too can perform miracles.

Pivotal Moments

Beyond the many firsts our cast of examples demonstrates, I also see deeper meaning in the actions of each individual. For me, these stories all share a moment from a person's life that becomes pivotal, and I see a pattern that suggests I too will have moments where my faith is tested.

The story of Abraham sacrificing Isaac is terrifying. I wonder why God would ask an old man, who has waited an entire lifetime for a rightful heir, to return to the brutal practices of false gods worshipped in Ur. The conflict in Abraham had to be intense. But he did as he was directed, showing God that he would do whatever He asked; he worshipped God with his whole heart and was ready to sacrifice any possession needed to build the kingdom of God.

The story of Rahab, while less frightening than Abraham's, still shows Rahab taking risks. She helps, hides, and lies for the Israelite spies, and then she marks her window, letting anyone, but especially Joshua, see her commitment. Rahab's change of character is greater than "that of Jethro and Naaman; for while the latter two did not free themselves entirely from a belief in other gods, Rahab acknowledged that [Yahweh] was the only God both in heaven and on earth."[145] Despite her profession, she is depicted as a virtuous soul in the third circle of heaven in Dante's "Divine Comedy."[146] She risked her life to save her family, and she displayed her new faith in God.

The story of Job seems unfair from the beginning, as he becomes a pawn in an immortal challenge between God and Satan. This is not a position most of us would volunteer for! And while Job does not volunteer himself, God does offer Job's righteousness up as a standard that can be tried. Job suffers losses, humiliations, and buffetings. And yet he does not deny God or His power.

Elijah's story seems to be common for many Old Testament prophets. He preaches and tries to convince the children of Israel to change. His initial lack of success causes him to question his abilities. Nevertheless, once Elijah knows the will of God, he does not falter but uses the power of prayer and God to testify about the one true God.

Each of these four people survived trials of their faith. In his epistle, James tells us that our faith will be tested. Perhaps he uses these examples to reassure us that we too can overcome trials. When you think of it, these four examples represent males and females; young and old; working and retired; those esteemed and looked-down on; those who are single and married; and those with and without children. They represent all of us. I heard once that each of us would need to have our heartstrings pulled just like God had done with Abraham. Knowing this, I hold on to a scriptural promise that God will not test me beyond what I am able to bear.[147] Have I lived through this moment of trial yet? Have my heartstrings been pulled? I suppose if I have, my life has changed and I have stopped asking myself these questions.

Four Keys to Freedom

James is teaching the lost tribes of Israel, and in their religious education, they may be like children; therefore, James needs to remind them about their heritage. James has demonstrated time and again that he has been trained in the Scriptures and that he knows the stories of his own heritage, so perhaps these four examples provide one more reminder.

As a child, I imagine James was taught by his father; he learned the four key statements that God promised the children of Israel while they were still in Egypt:

I will bring you out,

I will deliver you,

I will redeem you, and

I will take you as my own.[148]

What better way to internalize these four basic lessons than to connect them to biblical characters that we should already be aware of? In this lesson, James connects each of the four pre-exodus statements with one of his selected examples. Abraham was brought out. Rahab was delivered. Job was redeemed, and God took Elijah as His own. All of the statements, when added together, focus on freedom; they are the steps that God is willing to take to help His children escape from bondage.

Trials Make Us Stronger

I think there is yet another lesson that James teaches; this time it is related to his first acknowledgments that trials of our faith can eventually bring us to perfection. Think about the before-and-after events that each of our examples had. Before: Abraham moved away from his family of origin and began worshipping God. He learned about astronomy, business, and survival; he struggled with family members and even entertained angels. After: His wife, Sarah, dies. He finds a proper wife for his son, Isaac, he remarries, has six more children, and then he passes away himself. Before: Rahab is the sole breadwinner for her family, lives in the wrong part of town, and holds a scorned upon job (innkeeper or harlot). After: She saves her entire family from death, marries, and becomes a maternal progenitor of King David and Christ. Before: Job has experienced success in family, property, and fine things; he has time to study and has learned a great deal about God and His ways. After: Job is humbled by the power and knowledge of God; he seeks forgiveness and rebuilds his life. Before: Elijah's background is unknown, except that James tells us that he had passions like us. After: He has power to seal the heaven from rain and end the drought; he beats the priests of Baal, is hunted by Jezebel, questions his abilities, hears God in a still small voice, and is translated into heaven like Moses.

Does it strike you that there is not a huge difference outwardly before and after when our examples are tested? It does me. The fact that our examples are faithful, patient, or powerful does not guarantee that nothing bad will ever happen to them.

If we are brave enough to apply the lessons from James when our faith is tried, we too can become "perfect and entire, wanting nothing,"[149] we must realize that faithfulness does not protect us from experiencing adversity. But in our trials, if we can be more like Abraham, Rahab, Job, or Elijah, then we can reap the same ultimate blessings they did.

What blessings did James say these four individuals received from God? Abraham was called a friend of God; he was chosen, protected, and strengthened. James also tells us that Abraham was justified or freed from the penalty of sin. Likewise, James tells us that Rahab was also justified because of her actions. Maybe from Rahab, we are to understand that our past or even our present profession does not determine our future;[150] we all have choices, but sometimes we must be strong enough to publicly display our resolves. James uses the examples of Job and Elijah as parentheses around instructions to a community to guide their actions when members of their group suffer, become ill, or need help. Patience and prayer are the attributes that our examples demonstrate, and the benefits of their virtues are happiness and salvation.

Just as with Abraham and Rahab, who are both justified, Job and Elijah will also be saved from their sins. Now I don't know all the subtlety that surrounds the words *justification, salvation,* or *happiness,* and I am certainly unprepared to enter into a debate on their exact technical or religious definitions. But after studying these four individuals, I think that James uses all these terms to suggest the same basic idea that equates happiness, justification, and salvation with perfection. Based on his text, I believe that James claims that our four candidates were all made "perfect and entire" because of the trials they endured; they were counted worthy on Earth, and because of their faith, patience, and work, they entered the kingdom of God. This then is to be perfect and entire; prepare to live in God's presence, and then receive that reward.

Lyn Bair

Sorting and Bundling:
Integrative Questions for Reflection

What people do you think of first when the word *honesty* is mentioned? List their names.

What names do you think of when *courage* is said? What about *compassion*?

What do you first think about when *Abraham's* name is mentioned?

What do you know about *Rahab*? Or *Job*? Or *Elijah*?

Do you know where you come from? Make a quick genealogy chart (a family tree) of your ancestors. How many generations do you know about? Are you named after someone in your tree?

Do you act differently with your family and friends? How about with your coworkers or church congregants? Why or why not?

What one thing could you do to be more authentic in all the communities you belong?

Define the terms: *salvation, justification*, and *happiness*. Include both a basic definition and a more technical/doctrinal explanation.

Using material from this chapter and the scriptures noted, fill out the following chart.

	Abraham	Rahab	Job	Elijah
Firsts				
Pivotal Moments				
Pre-exodus promises				
Trials				
Blessings				

Lyn Bair

"CONTROL" IS NOT ALWAYS A BAD THING

…our task is to stay alive to the changes in that terrain and to trust the path as it appears before us, rather than try to impose our map on it.

—Joan Sutherland[151]

People I love have told me for years that I have control issues, so naturally I assumed I could write about control. Despite my so-called expertise, however, I have found the topic very difficult. Honestly, this topic forces me to confront a negative character trait, and I have had to think about the consequences of this behavior.

James spends a little bit of time addressing the idea of control. Chapter one clarifies: evil things occur not because of God but because of our own lusts. James spends time in this chapter and the next showing how man tends to be double-sided and inconsistent. Then James uses chapter three to write about our illusions of control. He explains how we think we have control over animals and technology, but in reality we have very little and cannot even control the smallest element of ourselves: our tongue. In chapter four he actually criticizes our behavior when we act as if we are "the judge"; in fact, James boldly reminds us that there is only one judge, and frankly, we are not that power. In his fifth chapter, James uses the example of Job not only to remind us to be patient but to remind us of how little we know and can do ourselves; thus we can control nothing. By virtue of the fact that James discusses control in each of his chapters, we claim the topic is an important part of our author's message.

Although the word *control* doesn't occur in Scripture, the concept is discussed in many places. James focuses on four demonstrations of our lack of control, despite our opinions of those actions. His first example is about our feelings and actions. James repeats ideas learned from David's descriptions of the different houses of Israel, specifically "of double heart"[152] and David's comparison between man's flattering lips and "double hearts," and God's pure words.[153] To strengthen his argument, James adds ideas from the Sermon on the Mount and the parable of the unjust steward that "no servant can serve two masters."[154] We may perceive choosing to follow Christ, but James questions whether our hearts and service truly demonstrate our convictions.

James next challenges our control of a small body part, the tongue. As before, he has employed several Old Testament lessons. Let's begin with a lesson from Job. In his grief of losing health, family, and wealth, Job prays and asks God to "teach me, and I will hold my tongue: cause me to understand wherein I have erred."[155] It is evident from the book of Job that our main character connects integrity with not speaking wickedness or deceit.[156] Remember integrity is a concept of being whole and complete; thus to achieve such a position we must control even our tongue and be thoughtful of the things we say.[157] James also may have used the scriptural passage found in the book of Isaiah in chapter fifty-four. To me this whole chapter compares the love of a husband toward his wife with how the Lord tends to us, the children of His new covenant. Through our commitment with the Lord we receive children, love, covenant relationships, prosperity, and peace. And to receive this peace, the Lord promises that every weapon and tongue against His people will fail if His people are righteous servants of the Lord.[158] Such statements, equating weapons with the tongue, remind me how harmful our words can be.

James teaches us next about exerting control over others and how we assume the position of the judge or God Himself. He exposes our partiality by showing our actions respect or judge others. He boldly reminds us there is but one judge. The children of Israel, indeed even the prophets, are reminded of this concept often.[159] James would have been familiar with the nature of Solomon, who at the beginning of his reign is humble, seeing himself as a servant king. Solomon even acknowledges his lack of understanding, for he asks the Lord, "Give therefore thy servant an understanding heart to judge thy people, that I may discern between good and bad: for who is able to judge this thy so great a people?"[160] The Lord responds to Solomon's desires by saying, "I have given thee a wise and understanding heart...."[161]

I like this story because it teaches me to seek a wise and understanding heart. I should desire to be discerning and see the difference between good and bad, right and wrong. But I should also allow God His right to judge His own people. In other words, I see it is my job to direct the course of my life and to choose positive directions and actions that will lead me to understand more and more, and as I react with other people, I should have empathy and kindness for them and their life choices. I believe this is the wisdom James encourages us to seek; this is the light (discernment) and truth (love of others) he wants us to gain. When James invites us to gain wisdom, he says, "If any of you lack wisdom, let him ask of God...."[162] His invitation encourages us to follow the pattern used by Solomon. But James goes further when he adds, "nothing wavering," or, in other words, be committed to the quest and don't ask for wisdom if you secretly want to continue to control others, because such a request is neither discerning or loving.

The last of the four examples James presents about the topic of control is about how little real power we actually have. As the source of his ideas, James returns to his understanding of Leviticus, specifically in the twenty-sixth chapter. In this chapter the children of Israel are reminded to keep the commandments they have been given. They are reminded of the blessings that God has promised them. They are also reminded of the consequences of not hearkening to God. The chapter first shows us how important we are to God. But then the chapter shows us how little we are "strength... spent in vain," "eat, and not be satisfied," "scatter[ed] among the heathens", and we "pine away in...iniquity."

From Straw to Pillar

Moses clearly points out our flaws but then assures us that despite our issues, our weaknesses, and our flaws God will remember His covenant, and He will bless us when our actions show we have remembered His covenant.[163]

In calling our attention to the philosophical questions of the past, James is reviewing a slightly different history of God's people. James follows the pattern that Moses uses so often to rehearse what marvelous things God has done for His people. James synthesizes the advice and counsel of the prophets to instruct me to control the interior and small parts of me: my heart, my tongue, my understandings, my judgments, and my opinions of my own importance.

It has been suggested, in the rapid pace of the twenty-first century, we should study how to deal with change rather than how to control the change that is occurring, and we should learn to adapt rather than remain static. When my computer does not do as I think it should, I try to troubleshoot the problem. In my experience it is rarely the hardware that gives me problems; rather it is small options the software allows me, the user, to select. Thus to change my computer's output, I need to carefully select the right options. Similarly, my outward appearance and actions are driven by subtle and small adjustments to my inward software systems. To correct and adapt outwardly, I must learn to adjust and control my inward decisions and feelings. Sometimes the adjustments I need to make seem dramatic and overwhelming.

James seems to be aware of this dilemma and counsels that we must be tried, cleansed, and purified, humble in the sight of the Lord. Again, it appears James returns to Leviticus and updates an older story. In Leviticus fourteen, Moses receives instructions from the Lord about how lepers might be accepted back into the camps of Israel. Leprosy was a disease affecting the skin; it was infectious and contagious, and people that suffered from leprosy were not allowed to live within the boundaries of camps or cities. Sometimes leprosy was a sign of sin, as with Moses and Miriam. In any case, it caused separation.

This chapter in Leviticus instructed Moses as to the rites to be followed when someone no longer displayed the outward signs of leprosy. The necessary change from disease to wholeness is divided into three parts. "First is the offering by which sins are absolved; second is that by which the soul is turned to God; the third is that of the fruitfulness and fruits which the one who is converted shows in works of piety."[164]

This story from Leviticus shows us the course of purification or conversion. Mistakes are repaired, commitments are made, and outward actions occur. To begin the process, we must first recognize something is amiss and not all mistakes are as apparent as leprosy. In fact, James is telling us our heart and mind and tongue are the parts of our bodies that need an adjustment. After making internal adjustments, we repair our mistakes. Next comes the commitment. This too begins inwardly between God and us. Often we make such commitments public, but the change occurs personally first. The last step in the conversion process is to outwardly show righteous works. This is where James cautions us to be sure we are not double-minded but thinking and acting in concert.

Applying these scriptural stories, I learn the very first step of change is to control things inside of me. Sometimes I go into control mode when I feel like my life is not proceeding the way I had imagined. Thus, I exert some extra effort to make things go the way my mind had arranged the entire situation, despite a myriad of rational flaws. One of the biggest problems, in the execution of my plans, is when I exert this control, I am affecting others and forcing other people to follow my script. A problem that often arises when I try to force things to occur according to the way my mind has planned is my script doesn't match the acts and scenes other people around me have written for themselves. I have only considered myself in the play I have written, with others being treated more as props than actual characters. In the end, when I try to control and reorder other peoples' lives, I become arrogant and believe my plan is the best not only for me but for everyone around me and is therefore the only "right" masterpiece.

When I am in this control mode, I also do a lot of evaluation of how others are doing within my play (and perhaps in their own); I judge others. In a sense, as the author of the script, I also am the judge of whether or not the plan has been followed well or not. This behavior rarely takes into account anyone else's review of my work most of the time; I would hate to read how badly critics have panned my play. Thus in my desire to have a little control in my life, I become the judge of everyone and everything within my sphere. I become partial to my way. Perhaps my biggest flaw is that I am trying to adjust everything outside of myself. James's counsel on this matter is for me to make necessary (even if subtle) adjustments to myself on how I feel and how I think. The control I am supposed to be exerting is inward and personal.

My husband often says: "Sometimes it takes a long time to arrive at your destination correctly." Our journey is not always about directness or efficiency. Our journey to focus on controlling our inward feelings and thoughts may take some time and may not be as direct as we would like it to be. Regardless of how long the process takes us, once we realize we are trying to force others to behave in a particular way, we need to begin the process of change.

When I think about change, I recognize no one has ever successfully forced me to change anything. I'm not saying that others haven't tried. But I am suggesting that until I decide to take an action, nothing will be different. In many respects, deciding to change is really a personal investigation about our belief system. It takes courage to personally reflect on whether the attitudes and beliefs we presently hold are helping us. It takes support from mentors and people we admire to risk such a personal review. It takes faith to start such a process. Most of us can identify our own negative attributes, but this process requires us to not get caught in a destructive and critical place but believe we are loveable and capable people who deserve something better.

A good friend of mine told me a story about a personal struggle he was having. So one day, he snuck away to the river by his home to do some physical labor. As he worked he was actively communicating with God, talking through events and situations, when to his surprise he heard his name. He paused and looked up the bank, thinking a member of his family needed him, but no one was there so he returned to his work. He heard his name again, this time looking heavenward for its source. Then he heard "no, out on the river," and he realized that someone was rafting by and waving to him. He later shared, *God just wants us to be at peace and focus on what we can do, but sometimes He has to interrupt our complaints by using other people to get us to be still and listen. Peace and quiet must happen inside us first before God can teach us what to do.*

Learning what to control (ourselves) is vital from James's perspective. Our author knows once we acknowledge change is needed, there will be mistakes we need to repair. This part of the process is also difficult. We must be humble and teachable to walk this part of the journey. James would say this is a trial of our faith and it takes patience. My friend said it took quietness and listening. James would also advise us to seek wisdom from God, praying for not only ourselves but also for others so they too may be healed. My friend said change happens inside us first. Finally, James instructs us to act on our commitment to cease controlling and judging others by being positive influences in our communities. My friend said he first had to stop complaining to make room to hear God.

To become perfect, then, involves a personal commitment to control my attitudes and thoughts, and to seek for wisdom. And at the same time, perfection requires my personal commitment to stop controlling and judging others, and to seek opportunities to serve. Sometimes this can begin with quietness, an awareness that change is needed, and then we can make room for God to touch our hearts. My inward intentions and my outward actions and interactions with others can all be more Christlike if I am willing to accept the challenge to become perfect.

Control is not always a bad thing, but we must learn to control the right things!

Sorting and Bundling:
Integrative Questions for Reflection

Do you ever try to control other people, events, or situations? How does this generally work out for you? What does your control-mode look and sound like?

What are the steps of change and/or conversion?

Do you have a personal experience with a personal change that you could share with someone?

Why is repentance part of the discussion about control?

How can you exert control on your inward parts (tongue, heart, mind)?

Describe the faith that you need to begin this change process.

Lyn Bair

BEING DOERS OF THE WORD

> People with integrity are those whose words match their deeds and whose behaviors mirror their values.
>
> —Stephen Covey[165]

James uses stories, examples, histories, and even imperatives to teach us in his epistle. In short, his epistle expresses to us what we should do and how we should be. He states directly, "Be ye doers of the word and not hearers only." This statement requires us to first hear the word and then learn how to accomplish what we have heard. Scripture is full of the Word of God. Do we always understand what we read or hear? Do we spend the necessary time to grasp the meaning of the words? Do we try to make the words real to us by experimenting on their truthfulness? Do we act as if we believe what the Scriptures teach us, or do we skim through certain passages, thinking they are flawed and/or unrealistic?

There is an Old Testament story that James may have been influenced by when developing his "be a doer not just a hearer" principle. This story occurs when God teaches King Saul an important lesson through the Prophet Samuel. Saul goes into battle with the Amalekites and is directed to destroy all they have. While Saul and his forces are victorious, they preserve Agag, the best animals, and many of the Amalekites' good possessions. Samuel reminds Saul of all the blessings he has received from God and questions his disobedience as to destroying all the Amalekites had. Despite Saul's rationalizations, Samuel instructs him that "to obey is better than sacrifice, and to hearken than the fat of rams."[166]

Samuel's instruction gives two connections; the first is between sacrifice and the fat of the rams and then in chiasm between listening and obedience. When a sacrifice is presented, it needs a fuel to be burned; the fat of the rams provided such a fuel. Burning a sacrifice on the altar "symbolized the consecration of the worshipper to Jehovah."[167] Similarly, when we have listened to God, we show our commitment and consecration through our obedience to His instruction. Thus, when James tells us to do more than simply hear the word, he is reminding us and updating this "obedience is better than sacrifice" principle. James's claim is doing is better than hearing.

To explore this "doing is better than hearing" idea further, let's go back through James's epistle, sorting each verse into one of four columns. The first column will include information James wants us to know: simple declarative statements. The second column will have information James believes we should already know something about; it is our background knowledge. The third column will include new information James wants us to learn and practice. The last column will be attributes that James wants us to have or to avoid.

Chap. #	Information We Need To Know	Activating Background Knowledge	New Information For Practice	Attributes To Develop Or Avoid
1	1, 9, 10	6,11,13,18,23	2-3,5,12, 14-17,20-21, 24-26	4,7-8,19,22, 27
2	5,19-20	1-3,8-11, 21-23,25	4,11-15, 17-18,24,26	6-7,16
3	2,15-16	3-4,11-12	5-9,14,17	10,13,18
4	12	4-6	1-3,11-17	7-10
5	1-6	10-11, 17-18	12-14, 16, 19	7-9, 15, 20
	16 verses	27 verses	45 verses	18 verses

The first two columns are about hearing what James is teaching, while the last two are about doing the work James believes needs to be done. More of the verses talk about doing than hearing, which suggests that more of our efforts should be about actively building the kingdom of God. Ultimately, however, I think James would say by practicing the lessons of column three, we are developing the attributes of column four. Therefore, for the purposes of this chapter, I want to focus on the very last column, for these items explain what we must become. Specifically, these include:

1. Be focused—don't waver or be double-minded (1:7-8; 3:10)

2. Be helpful—give others what is truly needed (1:27; 2:6-7, 16; 5:9, 15)

3. Be patient—(1:19; 5:7)

4. Be obedient—submit to God (1:4, 27; 4:7-10; 5:8)

5. Be authentic—act as a servant of God (1:22; 3:13, 18; 5:20)

In these attributes, James closely mimics a lesson Moses gives to the tribes of Israel. Moses taught, "And thou shalt love the Lord thy God with all thine heart, and with all they soul, and with all thy might."[168] Moses continued by commanding the tribes of Israel to put His words in their hearts, teach those words to their children, write those words, and keep or obey those words. Moses hoped his people would really listen to God and feel differently because of His influence. He instructed them to diligently teach and help others to understand the teachings and to write the teachings down so as to remember them clearly. And lastly Moses wished his people would be obedient and do all the things God had taught them. James's hope is similar.

James rehearses his be-a-doer-not-just-a-hearer plea (1:22-24) when he discusses faith and works (2:17-20). It is interesting to note that when James uses the word *faith*, he chooses the Greek word *pistis* rendered as "God's requirement, order, or command... [implying] acknowledgement of the requirement and man's obedience."[169] In this usage, faith is more than just believing; it is how man exhibits not only awareness of a covenant but an agreement to the terms of the covenant. James would have remembered the tribes of Israel agreed three times to the terms of God's covenant at the foot of Mt. Horeb, claiming they would do all God had commanded, and yet they reveled around the golden calf shortly thereafter. James knew it was characteristic for the tribes of Israel to focus on their works only. He knew that:

> ...it belonged to the defects of this false Jewish spirit, that, instead of regarding piety as a whole, proceeding from the inward temper of the heart and embracing the entire life; it held only to particular observances of the outward life, in which piety should manifest itself—that tendency to the external in religion....[170]

Thus, when James talks about hearing and doing or even faith and works, he knows our resolve needs to be deep, personal, internal, and wholehearted. He knows to hear and not do, or to proclaim faith without acting well were both flawed propositions. He knows this has been a flaw for the children of Israel since God gave Moses the Ten Commandments. James pleads with us to be whole, knowing our commitment to God must be whole and include both internal and external behaviors.

Another way James teaches us about being whole is when he instructs us to be part of a wise community. James reviews all of his five attributes with particular reference to our community at the end of his epistle, and he reinforces the idea that all these need to be internalized. But when he relates all of these characteristics to a community, it makes me think I do not become perfect by myself but in fact, I need others. This adds a new dimension to James's discourse on being focused, helpful, patient, obedient, and authentic, because now I need to help others develop these traits as well. It's almost as if James is saying we don't get to heaven and rejoice all by ourselves; rather, we hope to be surrounded by loved ones and dear friends, a whole community, the body of Christ.

Several years ago, I remember learning about celebrating the accomplishments of one individual with an entire community. I was the new leader of a local Boy Scouting unit. My mentor, Al, had told me how important it was to recognize each boy for the work he had done. An important part of this recognition was to find a way to involve his family members and his scouting group, so that he would know he was part of something bigger. Sometimes I wonder if Al was mentoring me in scouting or in the gospel.

Anyway, the ceremony night arrived, and I had completed all my preparations and extended all the necessary invitations; I was ready. Then I had one of the boys come forward. I invited his mother and father to come to the front of the room as well. I don't remember the details or the awards he received, but what I remember was the smile between father and son (and the hug later) as this young man was being recognized for his accomplishments. There were multiple levels of acknowledgement: his name, his awards, his joining with other boys that had accomplished this step before him, his parents, the audience, his leaders, and our scout unit. He had not completed this achievement alone; he had family, friends, and leaders all helping. Everyone was there to support him, but as we celebrated, I think each person enjoyed something different; perhaps they had helped, perhaps they remembered when they had received a similar award, or perhaps they too saw the connection between father and son.

We all may have experienced something different, and yet we celebrated together. In that one meeting, I saw the efforts of many boost the self-confidence of a single member. I recognized the scout had been focused on achieving a goal (some little patch or pin) and how he had been obedient in accomplishing each needed step in the requirement. I saw the end product of the efforts of his scout leaders and parents being helpful and patient as the boy learned. But the best part was the authentic love between father and son.

What makes the community or congregation so important? I think it has to do with what each individual brings;[171] it has to do with the worth of each soul and each member that makes the community or congregation a whole unit. One of my favorite poems is "The Touch of the Master's Hand."

Lyn Bair

'Twas battered and scarred and the auctioneer
Thought it scarcely worth his while
To waste much time on the old violin,
But he held it up with a smile:

"What am bidden, good folks?" he cried,
"Who'll start the bidding for me?"
"A dollar! A dollar!" then "Two! Only two?"
"Two dollars, and who'll make it three?"

"Three dollars once, three dollars twice…
And going for three…" but no.
From the room, far back, a gray-haired man
Came forward and picked up the bow.

Then, wiping the dust from the the old violin,
And tightening the loosened strings,
He played a melody pure and sweet,
As a caroling angel sings.

The music ceased, and the auctioneer
With a voice that was quiet and low
Said, "What am I bid for the old violin?"
And he held it up with the bow.

"A thousand dollars! And who'll make it two?
Two thousand! Who'll make it three?
Three going once? Three going twice?
And going… and gone!" said he.

From Straw to Pillar

The people cheered but some of them cried,
"We do not understand!
What changed its worth?"—Swift came the reply,
"The touch of the Master's Hand."

And many a man with life out of tune
And battered and scarred with sin
Is auctioned cheap to the thoughtless crowd
Much like the old violin.

A "mess 'o pottage"
A glass of wine
A game and he travels on.
He's "going" once
And "going" twice
And "going"…and almost "gone"

Then along comes the Master, and the foolish crowd
Never can quite understand
The worth of a soul or the change that's wrought
By the touch of the Master's Hand.[172]

The poem is a more modern rendition of James 2:2-4. The violin looks badly; it is broken and out of tune, and we judge its appearance and offer only a few dollars. Only the master violinist sees its real worth and with only slight adjustments is able to increase its value. Similarly, we judge people based on their appearance, and we are partial; only the Master judges righteously and sees their whole value.

Each of us has a role to play and talents to add to the community. Often we are our own harshest judges; we judge ourselves only partially and often recognize only what is lacking. But when we are doers of the work in our communities, everyone can benefit by our small effort. The same is true in the various congregations that we choose to be part of, such as school, church, work, service organizations, and/or political groups. We belong, and our contribution is needed to make the entire group whole. If we hold back or choose to be aloof and non-participatory, the group may never experience our value. We also may need to broaden our view in trying to see the vital role each member of the community plays and helping them realize how important they are to the well-being of the group.

During James's time, one of the hot topics was how God would rebuild the temple. Christ claimed He would destroy the temple and rebuild it in three days.[173] In a meeting in Jerusalem, James recalls the words of Amos that "the tabernacle of David, which is fallen down; and I will build again…I will set it up."[174] Here James explains that God would gather all His people and rebuild them. To the early church, this was something they thought would happen externally. Perhaps James is suggesting this gathering and rebuilding was first to be done internally.[175] Each of us is broken in some way; we need God to rebuild us. To accomplish this, God gives us community; He gathers us with other people. In these congregations, God has given us the tools to make His temple a refined and consecrated place of worship. The tools God has given us are focus, helpfulness, patience, obedience, and authenticity. We are to use these tools in our community to perfect ourselves so that each member may become a temple of God.[176]

James presents paired ideas throughout his epistle: wisdom and love, light and truths, faith and works, and doing and hearing. I think it would be incorrect to argue that each pairing is separate and isolated from the other. Rather, I see James presenting pairings as supporting details of his imperative that we become perfect. Thus when we know about one of the pairs, the second requires action. I seek wisdom and act to love my neighbor. I rejoice in the light and act on the truths. I feel the commitment of faith and obediently complete what is needed. I hear the words of the gospel and support others in developing testimonies. All the while, I am changing my attitudes and thoughts to be more like my Savior's, and I am acting in ways that demonstrate my resolve to be more like God with other people on a daily basis. Perfection occurs as I am about my Father's business.

Sorting and Bundling: Integrative Questions for Reflection

Describe how you study the Word of God.

Do you ever take time in your study to liken the words of the scriptures to your own life? How could this help make the passages more meaningful to you?

Complete the following chart.

	Personal Application	Community Applications	Next Steps/Notes
Be Focused			
Be Helpful			
Be Patient			
Be Obedient			
Be Authentic			

Why does God require both internal and external behaviors when we make covenants?

Read Luke 15:3-7. If we represent the sheep, how would you describe the worth of a soul?

How can God help you rebuild yourself when you are broken?

Write an action plan about living the five attributes of perfection: focus, helpfulness, patience, obedience and authenticity. What can you do today to begin seeing perfection?

Share your testimony of God and the power of living the gospel with someone soon.

_____

_____

_____

―

My study of the Epistle of James began with a query about my own life. I remember that "aha" moment of realizing that perhaps I had forgotten some important truth; I had forgotten who I really was. The five short chapters of James's epistle offer a unique synthesis of Old and New Testament teachings. In a way that is both concealed and open, James introduces the lessons taught in his Hebrew education and testifies of their completeness and wholeness through his knowledge and testimony of the work and teachings of Jesus Christ, his elder brother.

I am fascinated with the life of James. He was raised as a young man as perhaps the second oldest son of the family. At some point in his life, his oldest brother went off and started preaching. Stories from the Gospels of Matthew and Mark seem to present a brother who was confounded by the actions of his older brother. He even appeared to criticize Jesus about seeking personal gain instead of the glory of God. But then we read that Paul called James one of the "pillars of the church." What happened?

Jerome, a fourth-century Church father, references the gospel of the Hebrews to explain how the resurrected Lord visited James and they ate bread together. I imagine that these brothers also spoke at length during this meal. Perhaps this meeting was similar to the conversation two of the apostles had who walked with Christ on the road to Emmaus. Jesus and James discussed Scripture, the setting of the stories, the meaning of passages, and the foreshadowing and prophesies written in the Old Testament about Christ's life. They reviewed the events of their lives together, recalling family stories, important events, and various interactions with each other. They must have interpreted the meaning of different moments in retrospect to their present lives. I imagine they shared deep and sincere testimonies of the work of God. Whatever the actual events, James experiences a powerful conversion that Jesus is the resurrected Lord, the Messiah, Redeemer, and Savior.

Exploring James's message then leads us on a journey through the Scriptures and back again as he explains the truths he has come to understand. He blends his own knowledge of the Scriptures, the stories and lessons he learned in his life, with the message of salvation shared by his older brother. Many scholars have criticized James as not agreeing with Paul, suggesting that Paul is more correct in his interpretation of the Gospel of Christ. Not being a biblical scholar but merely a seeker of truth, I believe that the Epistle of James precedes Paul's writings. James does not reference Paul's work because Paul hasn't created them yet. In fact, it may be quite the opposite; Paul may reference the lessons of James, for he seeks James's counsel when he returns to Jerusalem. According to the historian, Josephus, the Sanhedrin stoned James about 62 A.D. Thus, what we have as the Epistle of James may actually be the first written book of the New Testament.

Skimming over the Epistle of James provides a few gems for Christian action. But a deeper study of the words and applications teaches that we learn wisdom as we seek to understand God's will for us, and integrity or perfection is gained when we act according to His will.

Is perfection still an overwhelming goal? Yes! But it is a goal that I believe is worth striving for, because in such a quest, I seek to apply the Gospel of Christ in practical ways. I seek to act on my faith in a loving God. I seek for light and truth. I make commitments, both public and private, to improve my daily actions. I recognize there are many people who can teach me important lessons, and I seek them out. I admit I am powerless over people, places, and things while claiming personal power to make small and subtle adjustments to myself. I am a daughter of God who has been divinely blessed with the ability to be focused on excellent goals, be helpful and patient with other people, be obedient to the covenants I have agreed to, and be authentic. It is in seeking authenticity where I strive to be the same person in all aspects, places, behaviors, and roles in my life so that I may gain my fondest rewards. It is in this work that I complete myself, I become more whole, spiritually mature, and I gain my own perfection.

ENDNOTES

1 Chieko N. Okazaki, *Lighten up!* (Salt Lake City, Utah: Deseret Book, 1993), 25.
2 2 Chronicles 20: 1-13 (KJV)
3 Martin Luther, *Works of Martin Luther*—The Philadelphia Edition, trans. By C.M. Jacobs, vol. 6: Preface to the New Testament (Grand Rapids, MI: Baker Bookhouse, 1982), 439-44.
4 David M. Whitchurch, "Discipleship and The Epistle of James," *Go Ye into all the world: Messages of the New Testament Apostles: the 31st Annual Sidney B. Sperry Symposium* (Salt Lake City, Utah: Deseret Book, 2002), 259.
5 Achille Camerlynck, "Epistle of St. James." *The Catholic Encyclopedia*. Vol. 8. (New York: Robert Appleton Company, 1910) accessed July 5, 2011, http://www.newadvent.org/cathen/08275b.htm.
6 Joseph B. Mayor, *The Epistle of St. James: the Greek text with introduction, notes and comments, and further studies in the Epistle of St. James* (London: Macmillan and Co., 1892), xli.
7 Acts 12:1-17 (KJV)
8 Acts 15:6-22 (KJV)
9 Galatians 2:9 (KJV)
10 Bruce R. McConkie, *Doctrinal New Testament Commentary: Colossians-Revelations* (Salt Lake City, UT: Bookcraft, Inc, 1973), 243.

11 "The Epistle of James," *Interpreter's Bible: The Holy Scriptures in the King James and Revised Standard Versions. Vol.12.* (New York: Abingdon, 1957), 9.
12 Mayor, The Epistle of St. James, i.
13 Anthony Selvaggio, "Hearing the Voice of Jesus in the Epistle of James", *Reformation 21* (May 2009) accessed July 5, 2011, http://www.reformation21.org.
14 Selvaggio, "Hearing the Voice of Jesus in the Epistle of James."
15 Brian M. Hauglid, " 'As the body without the Spirit': James's Epistle on Faith and Works," *Go Ye into all the world: Messages of the New Testament Apostles: the 31st Annual Sidney B. Sperry Symposium* (Salt Lake City, Utah: Deseret Book, 2002), 282.
16 William Ellery Channing. http://www.goodreads.com/author/quotes/949667. William_Ellery_Channing
17 Numbers 12:6-8 (KJV)
18 Joseph H. Hertz, *The Pentateuch and Haftorahs: Hebrew Text, English Translation and Commentary* (London: Soncino, 1960), 291: "House of Jacob occurs only here in the Pentateuch, and is a poetical synonym of 'house of Israel'. The Rabbis understood by the 'house of Jacob' the women of the nation. Moses is bidden to approach the women … as it is they who rear the children in the ways of Religion…It was only

offered their children as sureties for the permanence of the Covenant, that these were accepted."
19 See Exodus 19:2-8 (KJV)
20 See Genesis 35:10 (KJV)
21 Craig K. Manscill, "'If Any of You Lack Wisdom': James's Imperative to Israel," *Go Ye into All the World: Messages of the New Testament Apostles: the 31st Annual Sidney B. Sperry Symposium* (Salt Lake City, UT: Deseret Book, 2002), 251
22 Mayor, *The Epistle of St. James*, 179
23 John 5:1-16 (KJV)
24 Matthew 5:48 (KJV)
25 Gerhard Kittel and Geoffrey W. Friedrich, *Theological Dictionary of the New Testament*, Geoffrey W. Bromily, Trans, (Grand Rapids, MI: Eerdmans, 1985), 555-556
    1985: 555-6
26 Elizabeth M. Magill, "James Offers A Word for the Wise," Global Ministries – Genreal Board of Global Ministries, United Methodist Church. http://gbgm-umc.org
27 See Ephesians 6 (KJV)
28 Manscill, "'If Any of You Lack Wisdom': James's Imperative to Israel," 247. See also Exodus 28:3; 36:1-2 (KJV); Proverbs 10:1 (KJV); Deuteronomy 4:6; 34:9 (KJV)
29 James E. Talmage, *Articles of Faith*, (Salt Lake City, UT: Deseret Book, 1981), 96-97
30 Douglas J. Moo, *The Letter of James: an Introduction and Commentary*. (Leicester, England: Inter-Varsity, 1985), 61

31 See Romans 11 (KJV)
32 Moo, *The Letter of James*, 68
33 Bstan-'dzin-rgya-mtsho, *The Epistles of James, Peter, John and Jude: Authorized King James Version, with an Introduction* (New York: Grove, 2000), 28-31
34 Elizabeth Taylor Frandsen, "LDS Church News–Place of Truth." LDS Church News–Authorized News Web Site of The Church of Jesus Christ of Latter-day Saints, accessed 5 July 2011. http://www.ldschurchnews.com
35 *Courage to Change: One Day at a Time in Al-Anon II*, (New York: Al-Anon Family Group Headquarters, 1992), 76
36 Leviticus 19:15 (KJV)
37 Deuteronomy 1:17 (KJV)
38 2 Samuel 14 (KJV)
39 2 Samuel 14:14 (KJV)
40 Terrance D. Olson, "Agency and Self-Deception in the Writings of James and John 1," *Go Ye into All the World: Messages of the New Testament Apostles: the 31st Annual Sidney B. Sperry Symposium*, (Salt Lake City, UT: Deseret Book, 2002), 299
41 David Rock, *Quiet Leadership: Six Steps to Transforming Performance at Work; Help People Think Better–Don't Tell Them What to Do!* (New York: HarperCollins, 2006), 74
42 Rock, *Quiet Leadership*, 74
43 Bstan-'dzin-rgya-mtsho, *The Epistles of James, Peter, John and Jude*, 38-43

44　Whitchurch, "Discipleship and The Epistle of James," 262: the quote suggests reading of Hebrews 12:3
45　Romans 11 (KJV)
46　C. Brené Brown, *I Thought It Was Just Me (but It Isn't): Telling the Truth about Perfectionsim, Inadequacy, and Power*, (New York: Gotham, 2007), 80-1
47　Leviticus 19:2 (KJV)
48　1 Peter 2:21-22 (KJV)
49　C.S. Lewis, *Mere Christianity*, (New York: Touchstone, 1996), 110
50　Psalms 12:2 (KJV)
51　Deuteronomy 32 (KJV)
52　John Painter, *Just James*, (Columbia: University of South Carolina Press, 1997), 163
53　Matthew 6:19 (KJV)
54　Job 26: 2, 3, 10, 11, 14; Job 27:3-6 (KJV)
55　Job 19:25 (KJV)
56　Cardinal John Henry Newman, *The Idea of A University*. Martin J. Svaglic (Ed.). (Notre Dame, IN: University of Notre Dame Press, 1982, 27
57　Max Lucado, *Facing Your Giants*, (Nashville, TN: W. Publishing Group, 2006), 107
58　Ezekiel 34:25; 36:26-27; 37:26-27 (KJV)
59　Elaine Pagels, *Beyond Belief: The Secret Gospel of Thomas* (New York: Random House, 2003), 6.
60　Deuteronomy 32:20 (KJV)
61　Leviticus 19:36-37 (KJV)
62　1 Ephah
　　(Israelite measure)　[DRY]　1 Bath 72 Log

    10 Omer (manna) [WEIGHT]
    72 light ROYAL talents 72 mina
    (Babylonian meas.) 6 Hin
    [LIQUID] 4.5 maris 36 liters

64 Isaiah 66:1-2 (KJV)
65 1 Corinthian 12:22-23 (KJV)
66 Moses Maimonides, M. Friedlander (trans), *The Guide for the Perplexed*, (London: Routledge & K. Paul, 1956) 67: states, "Bear in mind that by 'faith' we do not understand merely that which is uttered with the lips, but also that which is apprehended by the soul, the conviction that the object [of belief] is exactly as it is apprehended."
67 In the New Testament, Christ says that he saw Nathanael under a fig tree (John 1:46-50). This may mean that Nathanael was living comfortably and contentedly and had no real reason to make any life changes. D. Kelly Ogden and Andrew C. Skinner, *Verse by Verse, the Four Gospels*, (Salt Lake City, UT: Deseret Book, 2006), 103: "Some rabbinical sources suggest that 'under the fig tree' is the proper place for personal scripture study and that the phrase may be idiomatic, synonymous with 'in search of truth.'" Nathaniel came to Christ because he was seeking truth and was surprised at the question Jesus asked not because he was being criticized for relaxing but because He knew that Nathanael was searching for truth.
68 Thomas Keating, *Meditations of The Parables of Jesus* (New York: The Crossroads Publishing Company, 2010), 42

69 There is a story that is used by Josephus, Strabo, Pliny, and Tactitus who refer to fruit that looks good to the eye, but when picked, it turns to smoke and ash. This fruit is called the apples of Sodom. See Hertz, *The Pentateuch and Haftorahs*, 900.

70 Hebrews 11 (KJV)

71 Dante, Alighieri, Allen Mandelbaum(trans), *The Divine Comedy* (New York: Knopf, 1995), Paradiso, canto XXIV: 70-78

72 1 Corinthians 12:4-11 (KJV)

73 Angel Naivalu, "Religious Traditions," Aspen, CO, 15 May 2011, speech

74 Bstan-´dzin-rgya-mtsho, *The Epistles of James, Peter, John and Jude*, 43-48 and Meister Eckhart, Raymond B. Blakney (trans), (New York: Harper One, 1941), 111: "St. Thomas [Aquinas] says that the active life is better than the contemplative, for in it one pours out the love he has received in contemplation. Yet it is all one; for what we plant in the soil of contemplation we shall reap in the harvest of action and thus the purpose of contemplation is achieved. There is a transition from one to the other but it is all a single process with one end in view—that God is, after which it returns to what it was before. If I go from one end of this house to the other, it is true, I shall be moving and yet it will be all one motion. In all he does, man has only his one vision of God. One is based on the others and fulfills it. In unity [one beholds] in contemplation, God foredhadows

[variety of] the harvest of action. In contemplation, you serve only yourself. In good works, you serve many people."
75 Keating, *Meditations of The Parables of Jesus*, 45
76 Hebrews 12:2 (KJV)
77 "Human vanity can best be served by a reminder that, whatever his accomplishments, his sophistication, his artistic pretension, man owes his very existence to a six-inch layer of top soil—and the fact that it rains" (quoted from Richard L Evans, *An Open Road*, Volume 3, Salt Lake City, Utah: Publishers Press, 1968, 148). I am confident that I am not the most important thing or being in the universe. I can see this going one of two ways: (1) I am therefore nothing, and whatever I do means nothing, or (2) I am small, but I am something, and who I am is important, and I can make a difference. I, of course, like the second option; I recognize my smallness compared to the universe and my importance in the lives of some. What I do affects others (many that I will never know), and therefore what I choose to do has significance.
78 Alexis de Touqueville and Gerald E. Bevan (trans), *Democracy in America*, (New York: Penguin Classics, 2003), 819.
79 James 1:2-4 (KJV)
80 Todd C. Penner, *The Epistle of James and Eschatology: Re-reading and Ancient Christian Letter*, (Midsomer Norton, Bath, England: Sheffield Academic Press, 1996), 141

81 Light/wisdom: James1:5-8, Truth/love others: James 1:9-11
82 Genesis 1:3-4 (KJV)
83 Isaiah 2:5 (KJV)
84 Story is in Daniel 2 (KJV)
85 Daniel 2: 20-22 (KJV)
86 Adam Clarke, *The Holy Bible...with Commentary and Critical Notes*. 6 vols. (New York: Abingdon-Cokesbury Press, n.d.), vol 2, pp. 344-5
87 Genesis 26:3-4 (KJV)
88 John 1:4 (KJV)
89 1 John 5:11 (KJV)
90 John 1:9 (KJV)
91 James 1:17 (KJV)
92 Psalms 85: 9, 12 (KJV)
93 Harvey Fletcher, *The Good Life*, (Salt Lake City, UT: Deseret Sunday School Union, 1961), 40
94 James 1:18 (KJV)
95 James 3:14 (KJV)
96 Philippians 1:11 (KJV)
97 Philippians 4:8 (KJV)
98 William George Jordan, "The Power of Truth" in BiblioLife, LLC (on line essay)
99 see Exodus 28:30 (KJV); Leviticus 8:8 (KJV); Numbers 27:21 (KJV); Deuteronomy 33:8 (KJV); 1 Samuel 14:4 (KJV), 1 Samuel 28:6 (KJV); Ezra 2:63 (KJV); Nehemiah 7:65 (KJV)
100 John 3:21 (KJV)
101 Dan A Oren, *Joining the Club: A History of Jews and Yale*, (New Haven: Yale University Press, 1985), 307

102 Oren, *Joining the Club*, 308
103 Hertz, *The Pentateuch and Haftorahs*, 141
104 Max Lucado, *Cast of Characters: Common People in the Hands of an Uncommon God*, (Nashville, TN: Thomas Nelson, 2008), 219
105 1 Corinthians 15:20 (KJV)
106 Referring to the opinions of Matthias Konradt in Alicia J Batten, *What Are They Saying About the Letter of James?*, (Mahwah, NJ:Paulist Press, 2009), 55
107 1 John 3:2-3 (KJV)
108 Stephen Covey, *Ordinary Greatness*, pp. x-xv
109 Matthew 26:36-46 (KJV)
110 Genesis 3:21 (KJV). Just as God provided for Adam and Eve he helps us with our needs, he "clothes" us
111 Maimonides, *The Guide for the Perplexed*, 386
112 Maimonides, *The Guide for the Perplexed*, 387-8
113 Tony Crilly, *The Big Questions: Mathematics* (New York: Metro Books, 2011), 191.
114 Genesis 35:2 (KJV)
115 See Genesis 28:10-15 (KJV)
116 Hebrews 4:12 (Oxford)
117 Peter J. Gomes, *The Good Book:Reading the Bible with Mind and Heart*, (New York: Avon Books, Inc., 1996), 20
118 *The Compact Edition of the Oxford English Dictionary: Complete Text Reproduced Micrographically.* (Oxford: Clarendon, 1971), 113.
119 Galatians 3:16-19 (KJV)

120 Galatians 3:22-24 (KJV)
121 Metzger, 267
122 Genesis 9:9 (KJV)
123 Genesis 12:1-3 (KJV); 17:4-8 (KJV)
124 Genesis 26:3-5 (KJV)
125 Genesis 28:1-4, 10-15 (KJV)
126 James 2:10 (KJV)
127 James 2:12 (KJV)
128 James 2:13 (KJV)
129 Many have criticized James for not agreeing with Paul about faith and works, but I think when you actually map out their arguments, both apostles are really giving us the same information. Faith in the Lord Jesus Christ is more important than the works of the Law of Moses. Paul goes to great lengths to make it clear that the law will not save us but that Christ is the key to salvation. We access salvation by having faith in Christ. James accepts this argument but additionally believes that we should be people of our word. If we say we believe and have faith in Christ, then our actions should demonstrate that we do have that faith, in short, that we should openly obey the commandments and the counsels of Christ.
130 Genesis 15:6 (KJV)
131 Joshua 2:11 (KJV)
132 Numbers 21:8 (KJV)
133 James 2:8 (KJV)
134 Leviticus 19:18 (KJV)
135 Deuteronomy 10:12-19 (KJV)
136 James 2:15-16 (KJV)

137 James 3:10-12 (KJV)
138 James 5: 14-20 (KJV)
139 Dante, *The Divine Comedy*, Paradiso canto XXV: 67-90
140 Genesis 7:5 (KJV)
141 Tad Szulc, "Abraham: Journey of Faith," *National Geographic* Dec. 2001: 96
142 Szulc, "Abraham: Journey of Faith," 96
143 H.L. Ellison, *The Illustrated Bible Dictionary, Part II: Golaith-Papyri* (Leicester, England: Inter-Varsity Press), 1980, 792
144 B.L. Smith, *The Illustrated Bible Dictionary, Part I: Aaron-Golan* (Leicester, England: Inter-Varsity Press), 1980, 441
145 Emil G. Hirsch and M. Seligsohn, "Rahab," *JewishEncyclopedia.com* http://www.jewishencyclopedia.com
146 Dante, *The Divine Comedy*, Paradisio IX.112
147 1 Corinthians 10:13 (KJV)
148 Exodus 6:6-7 (KJV)
149 James 1:4 (KJV)
150 Liz Curtis Higgs, *Bad Girls of the Bible: and What We Can Learn from Them*, (Colorado Springs, CO: WaterBrook, 1999), 166-167
151 Joan Sutherland, "Seasons of Awakening," *Shambhala Sun*, May 2012, 56.
152 1 Chronicles 12:33 (KJV)
153 Psalms 12:2 (KJV)
154 Matthew 6:24 (KJV) and Luke 16:13 (KJV)
155 Job 6:24 (KJV)
156 Job 27:4 (KJV)

157 See also: Psalms 10:7 (KJV); 12:3 (KJV); 34:34 (KJV); 39 (KJV); 52:2 (KJV); and Proverbs 6:17 (KJV); 18:21 (KJV)
158 Isaiah 54:1-17 (KJV)
159 See Genesis 18:25 (KJV); Deuteronomy 32:36 (KJV); 1 Samuel 24:15 (KJV); 1Chronicles 16:33 (KJV); Isaiah 11:3-4 (KJV); 33 (KJV)
160 1 Kings 3:9 (KJV)
161 1 Kings 3:12 (KJV)
162 James 1:5 (KJV)
163 Leviticus 26 (KJV); see also Nehemiah 5 (KJV); Job 35 (KJV); Job 40 (KJV); Psalms 78 (KJV)
164 Origen and Gary Wayne Barkley (trans), *Homilies on Leviticus 1-16*, (Washington DC: The Catholic University of American Press, 1990), 173
165 Covey, 121
166 1 Samuel 15:22 (KJV)
167 KJV, 766
168 Deuteronomy 6:5-17 (KJV)
169 Hauglid, " 'As the body without the Spirit': James's Epistle on Faith and Works," 278
170 Dr Augustus Neander, *Scriptural Expositions of Dr Augustus Neander: II. The Epistle of James, Practically Explained*, Kindle location 194-99.
171 1 Corinthians 12:12-27 (KJV)
172 Myra Ross Welch (1926), http://clankford.home.mindspring.com/Masters_Hand.htm
173 Mark 14:58 (KJV); John 2:19 (KJV); see also Acts 6:14 (KJV)
174 Acts 15:16 (KJV)

175 Hershel Shanks & Ben Witherington III, The Brother of Jesus: *The Dramatic Story & Meaning of the First Archaeological Link to Jesus & His Family*, (San Francisco: HarperSanFrancisco, 2003), 119: "In early Judaism there was a great deal of speculation about the destruction and rebuilding of the Temple and about the people of God, and Jesus himself had some things to say about this matter (Mark 14:58 (KJV); see also John 2:19 (KJV); Acts 6:14 (KJV)), as did Paul (1 Cor 3:16-17 (KJV); 2 Cor 6:16 (KJV)). It is not surprising, then, that the earliest Jewish followers of Jesus believed that God was rebuilding his people as his new Temple and that James was one of the pillars in that reconstruction." Pp. 119-120: "It is thus all the more significant that James himself speaks about the rebuilding of God's people in Acts 15:16-17 (KJV), under the metaphor of re-erecting David's tent" (quoting Amos 9 (KJV). James believes that in the future God will rebuild the Jewish tent, which will in turn cause Gentiles to come into it.

176 1 Corinthians 3:16 (KJV) and 2 Corinthians 6:16 (KJV)